The Mission of St. Catherine

Cross and Crown Series of Spirituality

GENERAL EDITOR

Very Reverend John L. Callahan, O.P., S.T.M.

LITERARY EDITOR

Reverend Jordan Aumann, O.P., S.T.D.

NUMBER 4

THE MISSION OF

ST. CATHERINE

BY *Martin S. Gillet,* O.P.

TRANSLATED BY

Sister M. Thomas Lopez, O.P.

B. HERDER BOOK CO.

15 & 17 South Broadway, St. Louis 2, Mo.

AND *33 Queen Square, London, W. C.*

This is a translation of *La Mission de Sainte Catherine de Sienne* by M. S. Gillet, O.P., published at Paris by Ernest Flammarion, 1946.

NIHIL OBSTAT
Thomas G. Kinsella, O.P.
Censor Librorum

IMPRIMATUR
✠ Edward A. Fitzgerald, D.D.
Bishop of Winona

November 22, 1954

Library of Congress Catalog Card Number: 55-6451

This translation is dedicated to the memory

of the Most Reverend Emmanuel Suárez, O.P.,

eightieth Master General of the Dominican Order

Foreword ✍

THIS WORK is not a biography of St. Catherine of Siena, but a study of her Dominican vocation, undertaken in the hope of gaining a deeper understanding of her apostolic activity. For, above all things else, Catherine was a Dominican and she constantly rejoiced in her Dominican vocation.

St. Dominic had resolved to establish a religious order whose purpose would be the salvation of souls. At the time it was a strange and astounding ideal. In order to realize it, he had to organize a mode of religious life specifically designed for the purpose. Consequently, he decided to add a life of prolonged study and prayer to the regular life of monastic observance. Experience had taught him that the apostolate is not truly fruitful unless exercised by saintly men of learning. Therefore, his sons were never to preach truth to souls unless they had made a profound study of sacred doctrine under the most learned masters and, what is equally important, were absorbed in continual prayer in the school of the Holy Ghost.

From the day that she received the habit until she drew her last breath, Catherine of Siena, inspired by the spirit of St. Dominic, had set her heart on fulfilling this program to the letter. She received the special grace of learning sacred doctrine directly from God and this doctrine, which was taken down by her disciples at her dictation, was later to form her *Dialogue*. One could say without exaggeration that Catherine's life was spent in contemplation and there is no need to search elsewhere for the secret of her marvelous apostolate, especially during the last years of her life. It was an apostolate that aroused the enthusiasm of her contemporaries and still astounds us today with its variety and fecundity. Consequently, it seems well worth the effort to explain this apostolate and such is the purpose of this book.

If only these pages were worthy of a saint who is the joy of her Order and the honor and glory of the Church! But no one is bound to the impossible. At least we have devoted all our care and put all our heart into the writing of these pages. If by chance they help to make St. Catherine better understood in the world and if they increase among the members of the Dominican family the desire to be more like her, to love God and souls as she loved them, then we consider ourself well rewarded for our efforts. May God grant that it will be so.

✠ Martin S. Gillet, o.p.
Archbishop of Nicæa and ex-Master
General of the Friars Preachers

Translator's Preface ✍

A l'impossible nul n'est tenu—No one is bound to the impossible. If Archbishop Gillet felt his inadequacy to convey to the hearts and minds of his readers the burning flame of St. Catherine's love of God and neighbor and the luminous quality of her apostolate, I am keenly aware of my own inadequacy to translate in all its brilliance the burning zeal of the author of this work. I can equal him in nothing, unless it be in admiration of the Sienese Saint. May she use these lines as instruments to challenge and inflame hearts to launch a new crusade against the secularism of our day.

The translation itself would not have been possible without the help and prayers of many who have followed its progress. I am especially and deeply grateful to Reverend Mark Heath, O.P., and to Mother M. Clare, O.P., who first suggested the translation; to Reverend Jordan Aumann, O.P., who edited the entire manuscript; to Mother M. Rosalia, O.P., who permitted me to do the work of translation; to Sister M. Joseph, O.P., for critical reading; and to all who shared with me their insights into the life and spirit of St. Catherine of Siena.

Sister M. Thomas Lopez, O.P.

Our Lady of the Elms
Akron, Ohio

ACKNOWLEDGMENTS

The editors gratefully acknowledge the permission of the publishers for quotations from *Saint Catherine of Siena* by Johannes Jorgensen (London - New York - Toronto: Longmans, Green & Co., Inc., 1938) and *The Dialogue of St. Catherine of Siena* (London: Burns Oates & Washbourne Ltd., 1925).

Contents ⁀

		PAGE
FOREWORD	. . . .	vii
TRANSLATOR'S PREFACE	. . . .	ix
ACKNOWLEDGMENTS	. . . .	x

CHAPTER
1	DOMINICAN VOCATION	1
	Earliest Years	10
	James Benincasa	14
	Lapa Benincasa	17
	First Vision	23
	Santa Maria Novella	36
	Early Penitential Practices	41
	Testing the Vocation	45
	La Mantellata	49

2	SIENA AND AVIGNON	57
	Siena	58
	Avignon	69

CHAPTER   PAGE

3   SPIRITUAL DOCTRINE 79

    Sources of her Doctrine 82

    Doctrine of Love 87

    Humility and Truth 93

    Hatred and Love 96

    Generosity of Love 102

    Holy Discretion 106

    Patience and Fortitude 112

    Heroic Love 116

4   FULLNESS OF CONTEMPLATION 120

    The Divine Indwelling 124

    Faith and Charity 126

    Mystical Contemplation 131

    Catherine as a Contemplative 137

    Mystical Phenomena 154

5   THE APOSTOLATE 162

    Field of the Apostolate 166

    Care of the Poor 170

    Nursing the Sick 172

    Solace for Prisoners 174

    The Eloquence of Love 179

    Catherine's Letters 186

    Reform of the Clergy 198

    The Crusade 207

    Avignon and Rome 214

    Epilogue 219

The Mission of St. Catherine

CHAPTER 1 🖋

Dominican Vocation

AT the time of St. Catherine's birth the Dominican Order, after more than a century of incomparable renown, was on the eve of undergoing a cruel, two-fold trial: that of the plague, which would decimate the Order, and that of the Great Western Schism, which would cleave it asunder. By ravaging Dominican convents the plague would precipitate laxness; by sowing internal dissension, the Schism would add the coup de grâce by sapping its vigor. Everything seemed to indicate that the Order of Saint Dominic, like most of the other religious families cursed by the weight of such disaster, would finally be dissolved.

But God as well as the Blessed Virgin, who since its foundation had showered it with signs of her protective care, were watching over the Order. In fact, just at this time, two stars of the first magnitude appeared in the Dominican firmament. With the help of their brilliance the Order would emerge from the somber night into which circumstances had cast it and would ultimately recapture something of its pristine radiance.

The two stars were Raymond of Capua and Catherine of Siena. The first was born at Capua around 1330; the second, at Siena about 1347.[1] However, it was only in 1374, when he

[1] In an article which appeared in the *Analecta Ballandiana* (Vol. XL, pp. 365–411), Mr. E. Jordan refutes the exaggerations of a cer-

was officially charged with her spiritual direction, that Raymond for the first time met Catherine personally. Catherine was then twenty-seven and she was to die six years later at the age of thirty-three.

The date 1374, which was that of the General Chapter of Florence, deserves all our attention at this point. For there is no other period in the life of Catherine which places her Dominican vocation in a clearer light. Consequently, the events of the Chapter of Florence put us in a better position to pass judgment on her life as a whole and to throw into relief the unity that lies hidden beneath its apparent complexity.

At that time Elias-Raymond of Toulouse had already been Master General of the Order for seven years. He knew Catherine only through hearsay, much good and much evil having been reported about her. For even in the bosom of the Dominican family, the virgin of Siena had her partisans and her violent detractors who harassed the Master General to pronounce publicly on her case. Not wishing to compromise his authority in such a delicate matter by making a premature decision, the Master General waited patiently until emotions were somewhat subdued and the issues raised by Catherine's doctrine and extraordinary life—filled as it

_____

tain critic who attempted to set back the date of Catherine's birth by ten years, in order to dismiss certain miraculous events as incredible and to attribute them to the imagination or the dishonesty of Raymond of Capua. According to Mr. Jordan, the date of birth suggested by Blessed Raymond of Capua in the *Legenda Major* is the only reasonable one. It results "from a combination of scattered data, does not violate any text, and reconciles all objections without offending any probability." He adds: "It is neither a proof nor a condition of sanctity to die at the age of thirty-three, in spite of the beautiful meditations that age suggests to Caffarini, the author of the *Legenda Minor* and the *Supplementum.*"

was with visions, ecstasies and miracles—had fully crystallized.

The General Chapter of Florence furnished him with an admirable opportunity to intervene and he summoned Catherine to the Chapter. In this way she would be able personally to vindicate herself before the supreme authority of the Order and to answer the accusations brought against her doctrine and her life as a tertiary. Catherine obeyed immediately and presented herself to the Fathers of the Chapter assembled under the presidency of the Master General at the Dominican Convent of Santa Maria Novella.

We are ignorant of the details of this famous audience, but we do know its happy ending. We know that the humble girl answered satisfactorily all the questions that were put to her, and with such humility and simplicity that the highly edified Fathers of the Chapter approved her without reserve and sent her back to Siena to resume her Dominican life.[2]

[2] Cf. *I Miracoli di Caterina di Jacopo da Siena di un anonimo florentino,* critical text with a preface by Francesco Valli in *Studi Cateriniani,* XI (1935), pp. 1–44. The fact that Raymond did not mention the decision of the General Chapter proves nothing. On the other hand, if the General Chapter had condemned the life and teaching of Catherine, his silence would be unintelligible, for he accepted his appointment as her confessor. In the *Legenda Major* Raymond praises the doctrine and religious life of Catherine. Is it conceivable that he would have done this without the least reservation if he knew that the Chapter had disapproved of Catherine? What is most probable is that the Chapter, recognizing the limitations of certain confessors of Catherine in guiding such a perfect soul, approved the appointment of a confessor truly worthy of her, Raymond of Capua. We find an echo of this in the *Legenda Major* where Raymond mentions the error of two confessors of Catherine in regard to her penances and in particular her fasting. Lastly, E. de Sanctis-Rosmini, in his *Sainte Catherine de Sienne* (Torino, 1930, p. 138), quotes an unpublished document which confirms the full absolution of Catherine by the Chapter.

They did still more. As if to put an end to all objections raised against her and to show definitely that they considered her a true daughter of St. Dominic, animated with the same apostolic spirit as the holy Patriarch, they also approved the Master General's choice of a Confessor for her: the highly venerated Raymond of Capua, at that time one of the most eminent members of the Order. Six years later he was to be elected Master General.[3]

It is probable that the choice of a confessor had been made by Elias of Toulouse before the Chapter convened—that is, in the spring of 1374—and that Raymond, who did not yet know Catherine personally, had welcomed the opportunity to join her at Montepulciano where she was completing a pilgrimage to the tomb of the Dominican nun and mystic, St. Agnes of Montepulciano. The pilgrimage over, both of them repaired to Florence, probably in May, to attend the General Chapter to which Catherine had been summoned.

At the close of the Chapter, toward the end of June, they

[3] The choice of Raymond of Capua as the confessor of Catherine is suggestive. It is probable that the Capitular Fathers, in the interrogation of Catherine, realized the incompetence of her confessors. At first sight the chronology of her confessors seems as difficult to established as the list itself. Among the best known was Angelo Adamari, probably the first, according to the chronicle of Santa Maria Novella. Later, in 1374, he took up her defense at the General Chapter of Florence. The *Legenda Major* also presents Thomas della Fonte as the first confessor, but he was her first regular confessor and he prepared her for her entrance into the Third Order. Actually, Catherine had many Dominican confessors, because the friars were often absent from their convent for the ministry or they were changed from one convent to another. She also had occasional confessors within and outside the Order and this caused difficulties in the direction of a soul as delicately sensitive as that of Catherine. To remedy the situation, the Master General appointed Raymond of Capua as the official confessor of Catherine. The General Chapter sanctioned this choice and the Pope himself, Gregory XI, confirmed it in a bull published on August 17, 1376.

proceeded from Florence to Siena where Raymond had been assigned as lector and where Catherine, now his spiritual daughter by decision of the Master General and the Chapter, would be able to resume her life as a Dominican tertiary under his prudent and firm guidance. She was to remain in Siena until God would call her to leave her retreat and, during the remaining years of her life, give the world a demonstration of an apostolate without precedent. It was to be an apostolate drawn from the very fountainhead of contemplation, according to the formula grown dear to all the Fathers and Sisters of the Order of Preachers, who claim it as the very spirit of St. Dominic: *Contemplata aliis tradere* —To give to others the fruits of contemplation.

Among the modern historians who delight in revising the biographies of certain saints whose lives seem too charged with visions, ecstasies, and miracles of all sorts, there are several whose method consists simply in accusing the hagiographers of having invented details at will or at least of exaggerating extraordinary events through a personal taste for the miraculous or with the well-intentioned aim of edifying their readers. The *Legenda Major,* a life of St. Catherine written by Blessed Raymond of Capua, her confessor, has escaped this rationalistic criticism less that any other. It has been denounced in scathing terms as nothing but a "heavy and dull recital of petty miracles." [4] Moreover, Raymond has been accused of writing it under the inspiration of mystic impulses rather than following the exact chronology of events. For example, in order to establish a greater resemblance between the Saint and our Lord, he had Catherine die at the age of thirty-three.

The critic who made this accusation believed himself

[4] The sentence is Fawtier's, quoted and refuted by Valli, in *Studi Cateriniani,* IX (1933), p. 142.

better able to explain the events in the life of Catherine by placing the date of her birth ten years earlier. But this arbitrary procedure did not succeed. Historians less obsessed with a fear of the miraculous and more solicitous for historical exactitude have shown in a peremptory manner that by antedating the birth of Catherine by ten years one not only does not settle anything, but he disturbs everything. On the other hand, calculations that have been made without any violence to the text and by combining and reconciling the scattered facts have demonstrated that it is necessary to accept the date suggested by Raymond of Capua—approximately 1347.

We are the first to acknowledge that too many lives of the saints have been written in an uncritical spirit and that too often accuracy has been sacrificed for the sake of edification or sensationalism. We even admit (and who would not admit it) that a historian as scrupulous as Raymond, intent on not asserting anything that he had not seen with his own eyes or heard from the lips of trustworthy witnesses, could, at fifteen years' distance, be mistaken in some secondary detail or could commit slight errors in dates. No human memory is infallible. But that is not sufficient reason for throwing suspicion on his work nor for denying its historical value, especially when it can be proved, as has been done in recent years,[5] that most of the facts he recounts from the testimony of his witnesses agree with other facts that are historically incontestable and which, therefore, corroborate Raymond's accuracy.

It is true that the life of Catherine, not only as recounted

[5] Professor Valli has shown the importance and trustworthiness of the witnesses invoked by Raymond of Capua, in particular the close members of the family of Catherine: her father, her mother, her elder sister, and her sister-in-law, Lisa.

by the *Legenda Major* of Raymond of Capua,[6] but also by
the *Legenda Minor* [7] and the *Supplementum* of Caffarini,[8]
the *Miracoli*,[9] and the *Process of Venice*,[10] is replete with

[6] *The Legenda Major* was written by Raymond of Capua between
1386 and 1395. Begun probably in the second half of 1386 or at the
beginning of 1387, the work was finished around 1395.

[7] The *Legenda Minor* is the work of Thomas Caffarini of Siena.
In its definitive edition the *Legenda*, like the *Supplementum* of the
same Caffarini, is posterior to the *Process of Venice*, or *Processo Castellano* (1411–16), from which it borrows heavily. According to P.
Laurent, who has edited portions of the famous *Processo Castellano*,
the reduction of the first part of the *Legenda Minor* and the first
eight chapters of the second part of the same work antedated the
early part of 1413, at which time the first section of the *Processo
Castellano* was put into circulation. Chapter X of the second part of
the *Legenda* would have been drawn up around August of 1413,
and the rest the following months. The prologue would not have
been written until after the complete edition of the work.

[8] Fawtier describes Caffarini as "the master builder of the formation and development of the cult of St. Catherine of Siena." Valli
proves that the entire first part of the *Supplementum* was written in
1411. Partly inspired by the *Legenda Major*, it was written primarily
to satisfy the disciples of Catherine who had reproached Raymond
of Capua for not having told everything. After the *Process of Venice*,
Caffarini edited the *Supplementum*, revising certain chapters and in-
troducing excerpts from the *Process*. The new edition would have
appeared after 1412.

[9] *I Miracoli di Caterina di Jacopo da Siena*, by an anonymous
Forentine, is the oldest source of information on Catherine's youth.
Two Florentine manuscripts are extant: one written at the close of
the fourteenth century and preserved in the library Mediceo-
Laurenziana and the other, dated 1485, preserved in the library Ric-
cardiana.

[10] Cf. *Il Processo Castellano* in *Fontes Vitae Sanctae Catherinae
Senensis Historici*, Vol. IX (Siena-Milano, 1942), pp. CIV–587. This
volume, published by P. Laurent and M. Valli, is of exceptional historical value. It presents for the first time the complete statements
of the witnesses summoned to Castello (near Venice) to prepare for
Catherine's canonization. To answer certain critics who reproached
the witnesses, Laurent states that there are facts in the depositions
that are not found in the *Legenda Major* and that those facts which

visions, ecstasies, and miracles. There is a veritable deluge of supernatural phenomena. What attitude should be taken? Granting the supposition that the historian as such must not be concerned with the supernatural, does this justify an a priori denial of the most evident facts that manifest it, however distasteful they may be to his critical sense? Evidently not. Doubtless, the historian has the right and the duty to submit such facts to the test of a rigid criticism in order to prove their improbability or their historical value, but once the existence of these facts is established, it belongs to others—to psychologists, theologians, and especially the Church—to probe their causes and to explain their origin and nature.

As regards St. Catherine of Siena, the Church has already passed judgment by imputing to her sanctity the extraordinary deeds of her life and by placing her on the altar among the great saints of history. Fortified by this official guaranty of the Church, we find our task simplified. It consists in revealing in what sense and in what manner the sanctity of Catherine explains the extraordinary aspect of her life, a life wherein the supernatural became almost natural for her. By virtue of living constantly in the divine presence, her soul inhaled God, if one may so speak, in much the same way as we breathe the air around us. While remaining truly extraordinary phenomena, visions, raptures, and miracles

---

appear both in the Process and in the *Legenda Major* are cited by persons who were eyewitnesses. Far from lessening the trustworthiness of Raymond, they corroborate it, for their testimony, although independent, coincides with Raymond's and substantiates the historical value of the *Legenda Major*. Father Laurent's statement refutes two extreme opinions: that of Fawtier, who doubts the entire work of Raymond of Capua, and that of De Sanctis-Rosmini, who approves of everything down to the smallest detail.

seemed to be the ordinary and habitual expression of her life.

Our Lord had said to His apostles: "If you have faith as a grain of mustard seed, you shall say to this mountain: 'Remove from hence hither,' and it shall remove; and nothing shall be impossible to you." And then He added that this is not obtained except by prayer and fasting (Matt. 17:19-20). One could not define the sanctity of Catherine in fewer or better words. She had the faith to move mountains because of the charity with which she was impregnated. So inflamed was her soul with the love of God that its slightest contact melted and dissolved all resistance. It seemed that nothing was impossible for her, because it was no longer she who lived, but Jesus who lived in her.

If, after having heard Catherine's case, the General Chapter of 1374 sent her away acquitted of all the accusations brought against her faith and manner of life, it was precisely because the members of the Chapter recognized in her the divine source which nourished her faith so that it might enlighten and sustain her. Catherine appeared to them as a true daughter of St. Dominic, a lofty contemplative whose contemplation, completely imbued with faith and charity, broke forth into exterior and interior action both in her private and public life.

The study of St. Catherine of Siena which we are undertaking here is designed to show precisely to what extent she was Dominican in her contemplation and in her action. To accomplish this it is not necessary to recount the details of her entire life. That has been done, and done well, by famous biographers from Raymond of Capua to Jorgensen. What is necessary is to search into the form and quality of her contemplation in order to penetrate to the very source of her activity and the secret of her love of self and neighbor as well as that of the visions, ecstasies, and miracles that filled her life. In a word, we envision a work of synthesis rather than analysis. We plan to throw into relief the dominant traits of Catherine's physiognomy in order to portray her true character rather than to say anything new on the subject.

EARLIEST YEARS

Catherine was born at Siena in 1347. God gave her the grace of coming into the world and growing up in a Christian family where faith was a living reality and traditions were patriarchal. Her father, James Benincasa, was a dyer by profession. Although he was not wealthy, he enjoyed relatively comfortable circumstances. His wife Lapa bore him twenty-five children, among them Catherine and Joan, her twin, who died shortly after. The latter was replaced by another Joan, who died in 1363 and was the last of the family.

Catherine was the only child that Lapa nourished with her own milk. Is it for that reason that of all her children, Lapa loved Catherine most? Doubtless, but also because she was extremely lovable; so lovable, as Raymond tells us, that as soon as she was weaned and able to walk and talk, her mother began to have difficulty in keeping her at home. All the relatives and neighbors wanted to have her with them. We are told that one literally had to tear oneself away from her, so marvelous was the precocious wisdom of her first words and so contagious the bubbling of her childish but eminently gracious gaiety. The widespread custom of calling persons by characteristic names led to her being called Euphrosyne instead of Catherine, as if to summarize in one expressive word the joy that emanated from her.[11]

[11] In Greek, Euphrosyne means joy or gaiety.

Raymond learned all these details from Lapa when she was eighty years old and, like most old people, she especially remembered the most distant events of her life with astonishing precision. In recounting these details Raymond is carried away by his feeling for Catherine and waxes almost lyrical. "Neither tongue nor pen," he writes, "can express the wisdom and prudence of her words. Only those can understand it who have experienced it. The fullness of my heart forces me to say here that not only in the living and real words of Catherine, but also in the simple influence of her presence, there was some unknown power that drew men's souls to good and made them take delight in God. Those who spoke with her no longer experienced sadness of heart, vexation of spirit, or painful memories; rather, there descended upon their souls a great peace, an unusual peace, which astonished them and filled them with a joy previously unknown."

To understand Raymond's enthusiasm, it is necessary to recall that he wrote those lines about five or six years after the death of Catherine, when his heart was still mourning for his spiritual daughter. He had met her when she was twenty-seven years of age, when the seeds of sanctity, which had been planted by God from her infancy in the secret garden of her soul, had already produced their flowers and were now bearing fruit. Involuntarily he associates his personal knowledge of the wisdom and grace of the mature Catherine with the descriptions he has heard of her childhood. As a result, he endows the child of six, a precocious child it is true, with the wisdom and spiritual maturity of the young woman of twenty-seven.

One may think that Raymond is guilty of exaggeration, but one also feels that he is speaking the truth and that the testimony of Lapa substantiates Raymond's personal experience when he states that Catherine's sanctity, grounded on wisdom and love, already radiated around her when she was only six years of age. In like manner, long before the light of the sun appears on the horizon, we see in the distance the white streaks of the dawn which announces it.

To judge fairly concerning the truthfulness and lucidity of Raymond's account of Catherine's childhood and adolescence, one must never lose sight of the fact that he unconsciously fuses the qualities of spirit and heart that he, as her director, personally observed in the mature Catherine, with similar qualities which had been observed in her as a child and young girl by those who knew her and saw her at work. Their testimony is so direct, so vibrant, and so redolent of truth that Raymond seems to have reached a point where he made no distinction between the beginning and the end of Catherine's life. He tells us that at the age of five this little girl, who was indescribably charming, already spoke and judged with the profundity of a woman matured by experience; at thirty, while she impressed everyone with her extraordinary wisdom, her youthful spirit still shone forth in her demeanor and in her discourse. There is no contradiction here; on the contrary, it is a question of a saint whose supernatural vocation was undoubtedly precocious, but from beginning to end it gradually developed as the child advanced in age.

Moreover, one cannot deny to Raymond the virtue of a sincerity which borders on scrupulosity in his painstaking consultation of all the witnesses who could inform him of the childhood and youth of Catherine. One must also recognize in him an art that is both difficult and rare in a writer: that of knowing how to let his witnesses speak without being unfaithful to them. He depicts them naturally and preserves in their testimony that personal note or earthiness which does not deceive. There is in these witnesses something profoundly human and at the same time dated and localized which carries one without effort to the period in which they lived, to the family background from which they sprang, to the very atmosphere they breathed, the house in which they lived, and the city in which their lives unfolded. They transport the reader to the city of Siena, which has preserved even to our day its medieval aspect but which is only the shadow of its former self as it was in the days of its splendor, when religion, family life, literature, art, industry, and commerce flourished there and which today is incarnated in its monuments and masterpieces.

All these things are to be found in Raymond's admirable account if one reads it sympathetically and without preconceived ideas. Far from being a "boring and heavy account filled with petty miracles," it is, in spite of the numerous personal digressions of the author, a lively and charming chronicle of a life which is as permeated with the supernatural as one could imagine, but which likewise remains deeply human. Each witness retains the characteristics by which he or she is easily recognized. Lapa, Catherine's mother, does not speak as does Lisa, her sister-in-law; nor Lisa as Thomas della Fonte, her first confessor; nor Thomas as Bartholomew Dominici, another confessor, whose testimony has been transmitted to us by the *Process of Venice*.

Above all, Catherine does not speak like anyone else. One senses her presence everywhere in Raymond's account. Some indefinable quality that is proper to her permeates the entire work. It is a harmonious mingling of the divine and the human, of spontaneity and reflection, of humility and audacity, of effacement and attraction, of tenderness and strength. Even when it is Raymond who writes, one feels that it is

Catherine who speaks. One seems to hear the echo of her voice in the words of her spiritual father. Through her, more than through her mother Lapa, Raymond learned much of the Benincasa family and thanks to her he was able to sketch with such truth and aptness the portraits of her parents, James and Lapa, of her sister, Bonaventura, and of Lisa, her sister-in-law.

JAMES BENINCASA

Let us first see what Raymond relates of James Benincasa, the venerated head of the Benincasa family:

"James is deserving of special praise. As Lapa told me, he was so even-tempered and so restrained in his language that never did an unbecoming word fall from his lips. He was a just man, giving no place to deceit and flattery, but fearing God and avoiding evil. Two things were especially repugnant to his shy and benevolent nature: slander and immodesty. He would not suffer anyone to speak evilly of others in his presence and above all to pick a quarrel. His wife did not have such patience and one day when she spoke evilly in his presence about one of his calumniators, he said to her, 'Let the man be and you will be better off. God will show him his error and will defend us.' This actually came to pass later on.

"The use of immodest language in conversation was as painful to him as slander. On this point he would allow no excuse, and his uncompromising attitude exerted such an influence on his children that the eldest of his daughters, Bonaventura, although married, became ill from hearing her husband and his frivolous campanions discuss certain improper topics in her presence and use indecent language. When her husband questioned her about the strange malady that nobody could understand, she replied: 'You can be sure that if this indecent language doesn't disappear from your home, you will soon see me die.' Her husband took her at her word, and in his house, as in that of his father-in-law, all unbecoming conversation was banished from that time on."

This portrait of James Benincasa seems to have been painted from the living model. It is as if Raymond had written at the dictation of eye-witnesses, as we may well allow ourselves to believe. For if it is true that Raymond began to write the *Legenda Major* at the beginning of 1386 or toward the end of 1385, and that in 1384, less than four years after Catherine's death at Rome, he had decided as Master General to have the head of the Sienese virgin carried secretly to Siena in a magnificent reliquary, it is likely that he took advantage of the feast celebrated on this occasion by Catherine's fellow-citizens to assemble all the witnesses of her childhood, especially her mother, Lapa.

At the end of the first chapter as well as at the end of following chapters, Raymond seems to confirm our conjecture when he writes: "All that I have reported in these chapters is known by practically the entire city or by the greater part of it. The rest I have learned either from our holy virgin herself, from Lapa, her mother, or from numerous religious and seculars, neighbors, acquaintances, or relatives of James Benincasa." Farther on he again cites Lisa, the sister-in-law of the Saint, as well as her confessor and persons who were living in the house at the time. Finally he adds, "I have learned from Catherine's own mouth, as I said, what she alone could have known."

How could Raymond have consulted so many witnesses unless he did so on the spot? And why would he not have taken advantage of his stay in Siena in 1384 to do this in earnest? He would want to gather as much documentation as possible, in view of the fact that he was planning to write a life of Catherine as soon as his occupations would permit, thus to spread devotion to her and, if the Church consented, to hasten her canonization.

Farther on, in the second part of the *Legenda Major,* Raymond returns to add several touches to the portrait of James Benincasa that he had already sketched. But this time it is Catherine whom he consults. This is evident in each line of the account and it can also be read between the lines.

James was ill and was soon to die. Raymond recalls how in the course of Catherine's childhood and adolescence, James had realized that his daughter had vowed herself with all her heart to the service of God. Since that time he had always treated her with a reverential tenderness and he continually urged all the members of the family not to permit any opposition to the wishes of his daughter. Thus, the love which united them to each other was ever increasing.

When James saw death approaching, he placed all his confidence in the prayers of Catherine, so certain was he of obtaining grace from God through her intercession. And that is what happened. By virtue of her entreaties, Catherine obtained from God not only that James should die a happy death, but that he should go directly to heaven, without passing through the fires that purify the smallest earthly imperfections. But this was granted on the condition proposed by Catherine and accepted by God—that she expiate in his place the sufferings that it would have pleased God to send him. Scarcely had her father breathed his last, when she was seized with a pain in her side and it remained with her all the rest of her life. Raymond tells us that she bore this suffering with an incomparable patience which was greater than her pain.

Thus died James Benincasa, the father of Catherine,

whom Raymond had not had the joy of meeting, but of whom he has, in a few salient phrases, drawn a remarkable portrait. Lapa, as well as neighbors, relatives, and friends, had recalled for Raymond the outstanding traits of James Benincasa when Raymond came to Siena to attend the posthumous celebration for Catherine. But perhaps it was Catherine herself who had best described James, simply by listening to the movements of her heart. For she had always loved her father tenderly. Even when quite small, when the outlines of her lofty vocation were gradually becoming clearer, she had found in him a champion against her mother, brothers, and sisters who, while loving her very dearly, intended to make her follow a path other than the one in which God Himself had placed her.

Never did she forget what her father did for her in this critical period. Up to that time she had loved him instinctively, so to speak, because he was her father. But when she was able to perceive and appreciate the high degree of his justice, frankness, self-forgetfulness, generosity to others, and submission in all things to the will of God; when she saw him emerge, after long periods of silence, to speak as the head of the family and to answer the objections they were placing to her vocation, her instinctive trust toward him changed into a tenderness that was spontaneous and boundless. The soul of the father and that of the daughter were intimately united as if to understand one another better and to thank God together for all the graces received.

LAPA BENINCASA

Lapa's temperament did not permit her to share in the spiritual intimacy of James and Catherine. She was a good mother who had brought many children into the world and dreamed of seeing them all happily married. Christian she certainly was, but in her own way. She sincerely believed that the best way of being a good Christian was to have a large family and to raise one's children well. Beyond that, which was not so wrong, she could not understand that God would ask anything else of her children.

"This woman," says Raymond, "had none of the sharpness of people of our day; nevertheless, she was skillful enough in managing her house and family." She was a practical woman for whom each of the small things of everyday life had a real value. She was very observant and nothing that went on in the house escaped her. That is why, at about forty years' distance, she was an ideal witness for Raymond when he came to Siena in 1384 and inquired about the actions and conduct of Catherine's early life from those who had known her at that time. Lapa still kept all those things vividly in her mind; it was as if Catherine's youth rose up again in her memory. Rather, her memory, like a piece of parchment, preserved faithfully its first impressions; it resembled an ancient palimpsest on which the most recent writing does not quite succeed in effacing the first inscription.

When questioned by Raymond, Lapa unfolded for him all the actions of which she had been the witness during Catherine's childhood and adolescence. Doubtless, she may have exaggerated some details or interpreted others in her own way, but one can be certain she did not invent any of them. "All those who know her," says Raymond, "know her simplicity, a simplicity which makes it impossible for this octogenarian to invent anything whatsoever, even supposing she had desired to do so."

As often as Catherine's father hastened to favor her views and to remove from her path the obstacles with which it was strewn, once he realized that God had destined his daughter for a special vocation, so Lapa, her mother, persisted in her conviction that Catherine should marry, like her other children. Indeed, she desired marriage for Catherine in preference to all the others, for Catherine was her favorite. Catherine was the only one whom Lapa had nourished with her own milk, and her childish graces, the charm of her small person, and her mature conversations were a constant source of amazement to those around her. Later we shall relate Lapa's attempts to gain her objective, the vexation she felt in not succeeding, and the complaint, so profoundly human, that escaped from her maternal heart when she realized that the contest between God and herself, in regard to Catherine's future, was not an equal one. God was decidedly the stronger.

One cannot catch Catherine's spirit, at once divine and profoundly human, unless he considers this paternal and maternal influence to which she was subject from her infancy and especially from her sixth year when her religious vocation was clearly manifested. Fortified by the support of her father, in whom a sense of the divine repressed any worldly motives that his daughter's future might arouse, Catherine was keenly aware of the truly human quality that lay hidden in her mother's opposition to her vocation. Nevertheless, she endeavored, with all due respect, to overcome this opposition.

Lapa certainly appreciated the meaning of the Christian life, but she was before all else a mother and, within the limits of a Christian mother's right and duty to dream of her daughter's future and to prepare her for it, she could see nothing for Catherine beyond marriage and a family. That is why she wanted Catherine to marry and make a home, to select a husband, bear him a number of children, and raise them in the fear and love of God. Catherine had too much good sense not to realize that Lapa's attitude was perfectly respectable from a human point of view. Doubtless she also realized that she would have to suffer much because God had called her to another vocation. However, this never prevented her from lavishing the most filial affection on her mother nor from giving complete obedience to her, as long as the obedience would not be contrary to that which she owed to God.

"Even if you die from it," said Lapa to her daughter, "you must take a husband." And when she once saw that Catherine had beat herself black and blue with the discipline, Lapa cried out, "My daughter, my daughter, are you trying to kill yourself?" Tearing her hair, Lapa lamented, "What is it that is trying to take my own daughter from me?" Then, overcome with pity, she lavished her tenderness on Catherine and insisted that she should get her rest and forego such harsh penances and prolonged prayers.

Who could believe that Catherine, in spite of her determination to follow her vocation, would be insensible to that maternal love? On the contrary, we have a thousand reasons for thinking that she did everything possible to avoid wounding her mother deliberately. Her affection for her mother was equally as intense as her awareness of her obligation in conscience to escape from her mother's determined resolve to marry her off in spite of herself. All her cleverness lay in the fact that by exercising great tenderness she gradually induced her mother to change her attitude and to understand that she should love her daughter's soul more than her body because spiritual goods are of much greater value than bodily goods. It would take a long time and much love; Catherine was not deceiving herself on that point.

A letter written to her mother from Avignon around 1376, on the eve of her return to Siena, is extremely enlightening in this regard: "Dearest Mother in Christ Jesus. . . . I have ardently desired to see you again, you, the real mother not only of my body, but also of my soul. If you love my soul more than my body, you will thus avoid all inordinate affection and will suffer less from not having me with you. On the contrary, you will rather find consolation in this and for the honor of God you would wish to share my hardships. In this way you will increase God's grace and virtue in your soul. . . . You know that I must follow God's will and I know that you wish me to follow it. It was God's will that I should leave, a mysterious departure to be sure, but one which has not been without fruit and great utility. It is to obey God's will and not that of man that I have left and whoever would dare assert the contrary would be supporting falsehood and not truth. . . . Remember what you did humanly speaking when your sons left you to acquire temporal goods; and now when it is a question of attaining eternal life, it seems so difficult to you that you say that you will die if I do not answer you soon. . . . Come, lift up your heart and your love toward that sweet and holy Cross which frees us from every hardship. Accept willingly a little pain here below to escape the infinite punishment merited by our sins. Seek your strength in the love of the crucified Christ and do not consider yourself abandoned either by God or by me." [12]

This letter emits the perfume of profound human tenderness and at the same time bears the accent of an exciting supernatural resoluteness. It is precisely the secret of Catherine that, without hurt or contradiction, she knew how to blend these two sentiments which are apparently so contradictory. On the one hand, one hears the heart of a true daughter beating with love for her mother; on the other

[12] Letter 240.

hand, one receives the impression that a mother is instruct-
ing her daughter in a lesson. More surprising still, Catherine had always acted in this way toward her mother, even
when quite small. Raymond of Capua relates an incident
which elaborates this point and reveals to us the soul of a
saint who even at an age when one would seem incapable of
such discernment, always knew how to reconcile in her heart
the obligations of her love of God with those of the love
which any child naturally owes its mother.

It was, as her biographer tells us, between Catherine's
seventh and her tenth year. Wishing to have a Mass said
in honor of St. Anthony, Lapa called Catherine and said to
her: "Go to the parish church and ask the priest to offer this
Mass or to have it offered, and leave on the altar so many
candles and so much money."

At these words the pious girl, who gladly performed anything that was for the honor of God, went quickly and willingly to the church. She approached the priest and told him
of her mother's request. Anxious to hear this Mass, she assisted at it to the very end and did not return home until
the ceremony was ended.

However, this did not please her mother, who wanted
Catherine to return home as soon as her errand had been
finished. Consequently, Catherine was not very graciously
received. Using a common expression of the people which
was applied to latecomers, her mother said to her: "Cursed
be the evil tongues that told me you would not return."
Catherine made no reply at the time, but some time later
she took her mother aside and with great seriousness and
humility said to her: "Dearest mother, when I carry out
your orders poorly or when I exceed your commands, punish
me so that I may be more prudent in the future. That is suitable and just. But I beg you, do not use my faults as an ex-

cuse for cursing anyone, good or evil. That is not becoming to your age and it pains my heart."

Such a remarkable manifestation of wisdom and affection in a child so young did not fail to impress Lapa and after having learned from Catherine's own lips the pious reason for her delay, she hurried to recount the affair to James, her husband. The latter, like Mary before the wonders of the manger at Bethelehem, blessed God without saying anything and kept all these things in his heart.

Now that we are familiar with Catherine's father and mother, and now that we know that both loved her tenderly, but each in his own way—James more supernaturally and Lapa with more human demands—we can better understand the strong and prudent nature of Catherine who, in order not to lose her equilibrium in the family drama which would be occasioned by her precocious vocation, would know how to reconcile from day to day the total love she owed to God and the respectful affection that God Himself commands children to give their parents. Just as the pilot of a storm-tossed boat must maneuver it skillfully in order to withstand the assault of the waves without letting it lose its direction or speed, so Catherine, to meet the tempest which her vocation would unleash, would have to be sufficiently gentle in order not to come into open conflict with her mother's plans, while escaping them, and energetic enough not to surrender anything that touched the love of God or the extraordinary life in which, by the express will of God, she found herself placed since the age of six.

FIRST VISION

It is not surprising that we do not know very much about Catherine's life prior to her sixth year, beyond the fact that she was amiable and possessed a rare precocity of judgment.

Blessed Raymond, who never misses an opportunity of praising his spiritual daughter and of tracing even in her tenderest infancy the signs of her future greatness, tells us that when she was very small she had a special devotion to the Blessed Virgin Mary and that even then she had formed the habit, while mounting the stairs, of reciting a *Hail Mary* at each step. To tell the truth, one receives the impression on reading this that Raymond could not have been familiar with the customs of that country, because he presents the details of this devotion as a characteristic manifestation of Catherine's piety when the fact of the matter is that the children of the time, and especially at Siena, were accustomed to recite the *Hail Mary* in this way while going up the stairs.

Devotion to the Blessed Virgin was widespread throughout the Christian world, especially after the thirteenth century, and it had been introduced in Siena very early. The lives of the saints of the period give testimony of this, as do the coins that date from 1260, which are stamped with the effigy of Siena and carry on the exergue, next to the phrase, *Sena vetus,* the significant words, *Civitas Virginis,* the city of the Virgin, as Raymond delighted in calling it.

All this gives weight to the accuracy of Raymond's description of Catherine's devotion to the Blessed Virgin when she was only five years old, but it is also true that such devotion, even under the form described by Raymond, was then very popular in Siena and in the Christian world generally. To cite only one example, taken from the annals of the Dominican Order, we are told that St. Margaret of Hungary, who died in 1270 was accustomed on each feast of the Blessed Virgin and during the octave, to recite a thousand *Hail Mary's,* accompanying each one with prostrations. Hence, the fact of Catherine's devotion to Mary is not to be ques-

tioned; but it was a devotion in conformity with the traditions and practices of Sienese families of the time, who used
it as an efficacious means of religious training.

Let us now come immediately to an event in the childhood of Catherine on which all the documents are in accord [13] and which had a decisive influence on her whole life.
We refer to her first vision, which she had at the age of six.
It occurred one evening in 1352 as she was returning home
with her young brother Stephen, after a visit to her married
sister Bonaventura, who lived at the other end of the city
near the tower of Sant' Ansano.

An old fresco set in the stone wall at the second turning of
the broad and rather steep steps that lead to Fontebranda
represents two figures, that of Catherine, kneeling, and that
of a young boy, her brother Stephen. Beneath the fresco is
this inscription: "When St. Catherine Benincasa, at the age
of only six years, was returning home with her brother,
Christ appeared to her above the church of the Dominicans,
on the other side of the valley, under the appearance of His
earthly vicar, accompanied by the holy apostles, Peter, Paul,
and John, and He gave her His blessing." [14]

According to contemporary documents, that is exactly
what little Catherine saw as she made the turn on the wide
stairway and arrived at Fontebranda, the famous fountain
situated not far from her home. The water still gurgles in
the deep basin and the women and young girls continue to
come as in former days to fill their jars with water.

"When she lifted up her eyes she beheld on the other side

[13] The *Legenda Major* by Raymond of Capua, the *Legenda Minor*
and the *Supplementum* by Caffarini, which Raymond quotes in his
account, and the *Miracoli* by an anonymous Florentine, all recount
this first vision of St. Catherine. The accounts differ only in a few
unimportant details.

[14] Cf. Jorgensen, *Saint Catherine of Siena,* pp. 3–6.

of the valley, above the roof of the church of the Friars Preachers, an exceedingly fair throne, decked as for a king, and on the throne Jesus Christ, the Savior of the world, in papal raiment and with the Pontiff's crown upon His head. With Him were the Princes of the Apostles, Peter and Paul, and St. John the Evangelist. Beholding the vision, Catherine stood still, struck with wonder and gazing upon her Savior who did so miraculously appear to her that He might win her love. Fastening His eyes upon her and smiling upon her with love, He stretched forth His right hand and made the holy sign of the cross over her, even as bishops do when they give their blessing. So mighty was that benediction from the hand of the Eternal that Catherine was rapt beyond herself, and though timid by nature, she remained standing in the open street, in the midst of the traffic of men and beasts, immovable and with uplifted eyes.

"Meanwhile her brother had walked on, thinking that she was following him, until at length he perceived that she was no longer at his side. He turned back and saw his sister far off, immovable and gazing up into the sky. At first he called to her but she paid no heed, and he therefore went back, still calling. When he saw that it was of no use . . . he pulled her by the sleeve and said, 'What are you doing here? Why don't you come?' Then it was as though Catherine awoke from a deep sleep; for a moment she looked down, then she said, 'Oh, if you had seen what I see now, you would not have disturbed me.' She looked up again but the vision was gone. Then Catherine began to weep bitterly and to reproach herself for having looked away." [15]

At the end of the second chapter of the *Legenda Major,* after relating many events in Catherine's childhood, and among them this vision, Raymond states that all these facts,

[15] *Ibid.,* pp. 6–7.

except the one about Catherine's flight from Siena into the desert one beautiful day and her miraculous return home the same evening, had many witnesses. First there was her early confessor, Thomas della Fonte, who lodged at the Benincasa home during Catherine's childhood; then there were a great number of trustworthy women, neighbors, and relatives.

It is evident that Raymond is speaking here only of ear-witnesses, in whom Catherine had personally confided and who had later spread the story abroad. As regards eye-witnesses, there were no others besides Catherine herself, for she was the only one to see, above the Dominican church, Christ accompanied by the apostles, Peter, Paul, and John the Evangelist. Her brother Stephen had meanwhile continued walking homeward and he turned back only to shake Catherine and wake her from her ecstasy. He neither saw anything nor did he know anything of what had happened. In the last analysis, the account of this first vision, whose details have been transmitted to us by all the earliest biographers of Catherine, rests only on her personal testimony. And what is the value of this testimony? That is the precise problem, and it did not escape Raymond's notice. In fact, twenty years later, when he was named her spiritual director and when her visions were becoming more numerous, one of his first preoccupations was to bring that first vision out into the open and to determine what he should think of it.

He does not hide from us the fact that he was often and in many ways tempted to doubt. "It occurred to me," he tells us, "that we were living in the time of that third beast with the leopard skin which symoblizes the hypocrites (Apoc. 13:2). In the course of my life I have met those hypocrites, especially among women, whose heads are easily turned and who are easy prey to the seductions of the enemy. That is what suddenly came into my mind. If I could establish with certainty that the prayers of the Saint would obtain for me from the Lord an intense sorrow for my sins, greater than the contrition I usually felt, I would have a definite sign that the works of this virgin came from the Holy Ghost."

Raymond then relates that, without revealing to Catherine his personal concern, he once asked her to pray earnestly to God that he might obtain this perfect contrition, but that he would not be satisfied unless he received from God full forgiveness of his sins. "I wish to be as sure," said Raymond, "that God has granted me this pardon, as if I had received a bull from the Roman Curia on the matter."

"What do you mean by that?" Catherine asked. Raymond answered that as a sign of complete forgiveness, he wished to experience extraordinary sorrow for his sins. Catherine smiled at this and assured him that she would certainly obtain this grace for him.

Raymond's request was actually answered the following morning during a visit from Catherine and at a moment when he was rather ill and confined to his bed. While Catherine spoke to him of God and of man's ingratitude through sin, Raymond suddenly saw himself in spirit before the tribunal of the just Judge. He had a remarkably clear knowledge of his sins, for which he was deserving of death and doom. But he beheld also the mercy of the great Judge, who changed this death into life, his fear into hope, and his sorrow into joy. At this vision he burst into sobs and wept so bitterly that he thought his heart would break within his breast.

Catherine kept silent and let him weep to the end. But as he wept Raymond suddenly remembered his request of the night before and Catherine's promise. Turning to her, he

asked, "Is this the bull that I begged of you last night?"
"Yes," she answered, "this is the bull." Then, touching him
lightly on the shoulder, she added, "Remember the gifts
of God," and left. "I swear before God," concludes Raymond, "that I am not lying." From that day forth, Raymond
was convinced of the veracity of his spiritual daughter and
of the authenticity of her visions.

As to the first of these visions, that of Fontebranda, we
have another proof of its reality and although it is of another
kind, it is no less convincing: the profound and radical
change which the vision effected almost immediately in the
spirit and life of Catherine. Raymond himself, strengthened
by the experience just described and the confidences which,
in his role of confessor, he had received from his penitent,
assures us that the influence of Catherine's first vision was so
great that the love of God flamed in her heart even to the
point of destroying every earthly love.

A year later, Catherine made her vow of virginity. Withdrawing to a secluded place where she could speak aloud
without being heard, and addressing herself directly to the
Mother of God, she pronounced her vow in clear and vibrant tones: "O most blessed and holy Virgin, you were the
first among women to consecrate your virginity to the Lord
by a perpetual vow, and you received from Him the singular grace of becoming the Mother of His only Son. I implore
your ineffable pity not to look at my merits, not to consider
my weakness, but to grant me nevertheless, the grace of receiving as my Spouse Him who draws all the fibers of my
heart, your Son, who is sanctity itself, our only Lord, Jesus
Christ. I promise Him as well as you never to accept any
other bridegroom and to keep for Him, to the measure of
my power, my virginity perpetually intact."

How can we doubt the testimony of a child of six, who

tells us that her vision determined her to change her life radically and to take no other spouse than Jesus Christ, when she knew, having heard it said often at home, that her mother was resolved to see her married, cost what it may, and that she would surely clash with her mother's will, thereby precipitating a family crisis and provoking against herself a war without quarter? It must be believed that what Catherine unexpectedly saw as she was peacefully returning home with her little brother Stephen surpassed anything that a child of six could imagine. Between that day and the next morning Catherine was changed, not perhaps to an old woman of seventy, as Raymond emphatically states, but into a courageous and intrepid young girl whose enlightened will would never allow itself to be thwarted by any obstacle, interior or exterior. Only once would she falter and that only for a fleeting moment and under the influence of her older sister Bonaventura who, wishing to second the plans of her mother, played on Catherine's affection for her to tempt her to change her mind and to renounce her vow of virginity.

Let us try to understand what she saw over the church of the Dominicans when, letting her brother go on his way and insensible to the noise and traffic of the square of Fontebranda, she suddenly stopped, stood still, and, with eyes fixed on the miraculous apparition, fell into an ecstasy. First, she saw God in the person of Jesus, His only Son, who for love of men and to atone for their sins became man in order to die on the cross and shed His blood to the very last drop. Those who are acquainted with the teaching of St. Catherine as contained in her numerous letters and her *Dialogue* cannot for an instant doubt that from the time of that first encounter Catherine saw above all else in Jesus Christ the

Savior on whom all her life she would focus all her love. At the age of seven she would choose Him as her only spouse and by a total offering of herself, she would suffer with Him and like Him for the salvation of sinners up to her final breath. Without speaking of the divine grace from within, which enabled her to penetrate the deep significance of the apparition, she understood from certain exterior signs what Jesus Christ wished of her as He smiled on her and blessed her. He was inviting her to consecrate herself to Him and to His Church for the salvation of souls.

Let us recall that He appeared to her with the tiara on His head and clothed in pontifical robes, in the role of Pope and Head of the Church, of that mystical body of which He is head and of which the faithful are members. Moreover, He was accompanied by His three greatest apostles: Peter his vicar and the visible head of the Church—the "sweet Christ on earth" as Catherine would say later when speaking of the Pope—to whom Jesus by His supreme authority had confided His lambs and His sheep; [16] Paul, Apostle to the Gentiles, who having been converted by Jesus Christ, gave himself completely to Him, trembling with love and ardor and boasting proudly of knowing only Jesus and Jesus Crucified, of living under His inspiration only to work for the salvation of souls, according to these magnificent words that he wrote to the Romans: "All the commandments are contained in this one sentence: Thou shalt love thy neighbor as thyself. . . . Love is the fullness of the law"; [17] and lastly, John the beloved disciple, whose head had rested on the heart of Jesus and who, during the last years of his life, when he could no longer write nor preach,

[16] John. 21:15.
[17] Rom. 13:9–10.

repeated continually to his disciples, "Love one another," while adding, "This is the commandment of the Lord; if you keep this one commandment it will suffice." [18]

The vision was perfectly clear and Catherine could not be mistaken. The Savior, accompanied by the three apostles, had come to make known her special vocation: she must consecrate her life to the apostolate. Her heart, inflamed with the love of Jesus Christ, would also burn with love of His Church and would give itself entirely to the salvation of souls.

But where and in what manner? Apparently, in the Order of St. Dominic and following the spirit of its founder. That is the reason why Jesus appeared to her above the Church of the Dominicans, as if to say to her: "My daughter, it is My will that one day you should be a part of this essentially apostolic Order. A century ago, under My inspiration, Dominic founded it for the sole purpose of saving souls, of rescuing them from heresy, and of revivifying their faith and their love of God. Since that time his sons have accomplished wondrous results and have spread over all Europe and even to the Far East. While they preach and fight the good fight, holy women clothed in the same white habit pray day and night and do penance for their intention in monasteries far removed from the noise and distractions of the world. Others, while remaining in the world, wear the habit of the Friars Preachers under the name of tertiaries and collaborate with them, under their direction, for the salvation of souls. There are some tertiaries here in Siena who, without realizing it, are waiting for you."

Assuredly, Jesus did not speak in such a precise manner on the day of the vision; He was content to smile on her lovingly and to bless her. But this message was virtually con-

[18] Cf. St. Jerome's commentary on the Epistle to the Galatians, 6:10.

tained in the fact that the apparition appeared over the church of the Dominicans. Catherine herself was not long in perceiving this although she had not had the least intuition of it at the moment. Actually, when she made her vow of virginity less than a year after this remarkable vision, the divine love that was ignited in her and prompted her to mortify herself and take the discipline, after the example of the fathers of the desert and countless saints, in particular of St. Dominic, also inflamed her heart with a love for souls. She began to love in particular the saints who had worked for the salvation of souls. It was then, Raymond tells us, that the Lord made known to her through revelation that the holy Patriarch Dominic had founded the Order of Friars Preachers for the defense of the faith.

There has been great discussion concerning this particular passage, and especially of the word "revelation," which is used here to designate the manner in which Catherine became acquainted with the Order of Preachers. Certain commentators have taken this expression literally, as if God in person and without an intermediary had told her the story of St. Dominic. Others have explained that she had learned it through a kindly and divine inspiration which enabled her to extract from the lives of the saints the economy, the *raison d'être,* the end, and the method to be followed in the ascetical life. Such interpretations either presume too much or concede too little.

We shall not do Blessed Raymond of Capua the injury of believing, as some have done, that in the space of ten pages in his account he would contradict himself. In fact, in the second chapter of his book, after having described the vision above the church of the Dominicans and having noted the intense reaction which took place in Catherine's heart and spirit soon after, Raymond observes that at that moment Catherine, under the influence of the Holy Ghost, learned directly from the Lord the lives and customs of the fathers of the desert and of several saints, among them, that of St. Dominic.

We understand exactly what the author means to say when he states that Catherine learned something directly from the Savior and when he refers later on to some kind of a revelation. He expressly states that Catherine received this knowledge solely under the influence of the Holy Ghost; in other words, under the inspiration of the Holy Ghost. There is no need to twist the text in order to give it a clear meaning. Neither is it necessary to have recourse to revelations properly so called, in which God would have appeared in person to Catherine to teach her what He wished her to know, as a teacher would instruct a favorite pupil.

After the first vision at the age of six, Catherine was concerned only with mortifying herself and doing penance in order to prove her love of Jesus Christ. Then the Holy Spirit inspired her to imitate the fathers of the desert and certain saints, including St. Dominic, in their mortifications and spirit of penance.

A year later, after having made a vow of virginity, Catherine felt herself overwhelmed with love and zeal for souls. Again the Holy Ghost inspires her, this time to have recourse to St. Dominic, and by a special grace of enlightenment He makes her understand that this holy Patriarch had founded the Order of Friars Preachers especially for the defense of the faith and the salvation of souls.

Does this mean that before the double inspiration by the Holy Ghost Catherine had never heard of the fathers of the desert or of St. Dominic? We may think so, if we take the word revelation in a literal sense and overlook the qualifications which Raymond himself added to it. But is it credible that in a family as Christian as that of the Benincasa's, with whom Catherine's first confessor Thomas della Fonte had lived and grown up, so to speak, and which he as well as religious of other orders must have visited often during Catherine's childhood, that little Catherine, who could neither read nor write, had never heard about the fathers of the desert, the lives of the saints, or of St. Dominic? Or, if she had heard of them, that she paid no attention to them and retained nothing of what she had heard? Certainly not; but what she had heard about them in the course of family conversations or during the family prayers and readings did not suffice to reveal to her either the depth of their spirit of penance or the quality of their apostolic zeal. So it was that at least two times, according to Raymond, these things were revealed to her under the influence of the Holy Ghost.

As regards St. Dominic in particular, the case is clear. Raymond tells us that at the age of six and under the influence of the Holy Ghost Catherine succeeded in knowing him well and she comprehended his spirit of penance. When, a year later, God revealed to Catherine (to use a favorite expression of Raymond) that St. Dominic had founded his Order expressly for the salvation of souls, it was not to teach her what she had already learned the preceding year, but to draw her attention to the special mission of the Friars Preachers and to the apostolic spirit of the Order at a time when Catherine felt her heart transported by a love of souls and zeal for their salvation.

This explanation of the text of Raymond of Capua seems most in conformity with his thought and his own words. In speaking of his spiritual daughter and of the graces which God showered upon her, the writer had not thought for a moment that six centuries later a swarm of critics would pounce upon him to pick his expressions to pieces and adapt them to their own way of thinking. His great preoccupation had been to show how God, from Catherine's earliest childhood, had enlightened her by His inspirations and filled her with the Holy Ghost in order to prepare her slowly but progressively for her great vocation.

Thanks to Raymond, we are able to witness the harmonious development of Catherine's Dominican vocation and follow its slightest progress. We see how, after the apparition of the Savior and His chosen apostles above the church of the Friars Preachers, God introduces her, by means of select graces, to the life of St. Dominic, revealing to her his spirit of penance and his apostolic zeal. Then later, in the midst of family trials which became more and more severe, St. Dominic himself would appear to her and show her the habit of the Order with which she would soon be clothed.

What is certain is that from the time that Catherine perceived the apostolic vocation of the Dominican Order in the manner we have described, she set herself to learn more about it and to be more closely associated with it. As Raymond tells us, she began to revere this Order so much that when she would see the Dominican friars pass in the street before the door of her home, she would observe the places where they had walked and after they had passed, she would kiss their footprints with humility and devotion. From that time she began to experience an ever-increasing desire to enter this Order so that with the Friars and like them she could be useful to souls.

SANTA MARIA NOVELLA

In Catherine's time the convent and church of the Dominicans in Siena rose up like a fortress above the esplanade of Camporegio, so that its compact and harmonious bulk dominated the narrow valley in which Fontebranda was located. When leaving her father's house, Catherine had only to lift her eyes to see the convent and church of the Dominicans.

The convent was founded in 1226, only five years after the death of Saint Dominic, and it soon became one of the principal centers of the spiritual and intellectual life of the Order. Toward the middle of the fourteenth century its General Studium was very famous, not so much for the number of its students as for the renown of its professors, many of whom had attended the most famous universities of Europe. We have already mentioned that Raymond of Capua, the future confessor of Catherine, was assigned to Siena as a lector in 1374.

In 1354, when Catherine was dreaming of entering the Dominican Order and even hoped, if it were possible, to live in the Dominican Convent at Siena, a few of the religious such as Fra Angelo Ademari and Fra Bartholomew Mantucci had a certain influence over her. The chronicle of Santa Maria Novella, which is of a later period but is drawn from ancient sources, tells us that in 1352 Catherine, who was then not more than five years old, went to confession to Fra Angelo Adimari. It is certain that at that time Fra Angelo was living at the convent in Siena. Therefore, he was chronologically the first confessor of Catherine. He was the one in whom she confided when she was quite small (*fanciullina,* the chronicle emphatically states) and from her earliest years *(da' primi anni).*

However, Raymond of Capua names Father Thomas della Fonte as the first confessor of Catherine. Which shall we believe, the chronicle or Raymond? The discussion of this question has already caused much ink to flow. In order not to weigh down this work uselessly, we shall content ourselves with a statement of the problem and what appears to us to be the most plausible solution.

In his deposition at the *Processo Castellano* (incorrectly called the *Process of Venice*), Thomas of Siena (Caffarini) names the following as confessors of Catherine: Thomas della Fonte (who died August 22, 1390); Bartholomew Mantucci (who died August 4, 1415); Bartholomew Dominici (who died July 3, 1415), and Raymond of Capua, who was elected Master General of the Order shortly after Catherine's death. Raymond speaks of Thomas della Fonte as the first confessor of Catherine, but the chronicle of Santa Maria Novella states that Catherine's first confessor was Angelo Adimari.

In 1352 Catherine was about five years old and it is certain that at that date Adimari was at Siena. It is probable that he was her first confessor. At that time Thomas della Fonte was only fifteen years old and was living at the Benincasa home. He did not enter the Dominican Order until he was over twenty. How long Adimari remained at Siena and heard Catherine's confessions we do not know, but we do know that another Dominican, Bartholomew Mantucci, was the director of the Third Order or the *Mantellate* when Catherine took the habit and that he also was one of her confessors. One could assume that Bartholomew Mantucci followed Adimari as Catherine's confessor when the latter left Siena at the close of 1352. Granting this hypothesis, which seems plausible, how could Raymond say that Thomas della Fonte, who succeeded Mantucci, had been the first confessor of Catherine when in reality he had been the third?

The difficulty can be resolved without hair-splitting. Raymond, who had been named Catherine's confessor and spiritual director by the Master General, was her official and ordinary confessor. It is probable that Raymond refers to Thomas della Fonte also as an official confessor, for della Fonte had not only confessed but also directed Catherine until the appointment of Raymond. In this sense he would have been Catherine's first spiritual director and her ordinary confessor. The others had been only occasional confessors. We are led to this conclusion by the fact that Fra Bartholomew Dominici, also named by Caffarini as one of Catherine's confessors, only heard Catherine's confessions when della Fonte was absent. Raymond himself gives us this detail in the *Legenda Major*.

But when did Thomas della Fonte become the official confessor and director of Catherine? Bartholomew Dominici helps us to answer this. He tells us that he knew Catherine in 1368, when she had already been wearing the habit of the Sisters of Penance of St. Dominic for several years. This data agrees on all points with Raymond, who tells us that Catherine received the habit shortly after the death of Bonaventura, that is, shortly after 1362. How old was Thomas della Fonte at that time? We know that he was born in 1337, ten years before Catherine, and that he lived in the Benincasa home. In 1363, when Catherine received the habit, Thomas was about 26. But Bartholomew Dominici tells us that he entered the Dominican novitiate late—after his twentieth birthday. Bartholomew entered at the same time, but at the age of thirteen. Hence, Thomas della Fonte was at most a novice by 1357. Granted that after his novitiate he had made his regular theological studies, it seems he would have been able to begin his ministry around 1362. And since, according to Bartholomew, he was already Catherine's confessor in 1368, it is between these two dates that he was destined for this delicate task.

Catherine was very much discussed at the time. Thomas

della Fonte, we are told, was not a great theologian, but he was an excellent religious and possessed sound judgment. Doubtless that is why he was chosen as Catherine's confessor, and also because he had known Catherine and her family since his childhood. There is much likelihood in all this and one finds no contradiction. Catherine had many other occasional confessors, if one can believe all those who praise themselves as having been her confessors. Raymond rightly characterizes them as imprudent, for they have injured Catherine's reputation by talking too much about what they know or talking still more about what they do not know. It is mainly because of them that Catherine was summoned to the General Chapter in 1374 and it was to put an end to their gossip that Raymond was named as the confessor-director of Catherine.

Whatever may be said apart from this solution, which does not force any text and harmonizes with other incidents and dates that are indisputable, it is certain that from her earliest years, at least from the age of five, Catherine already knew the way to the church and convent of the Friars Preachers. To reach Santa Maria Novella it was necessary to ascend from the Fontebranda along the steep and winding steps of red brick, which took one's breath away. By the time Catherine was seven years old she could climb the steps so easily that it was like playing a game. At home, also, she would run up the stairs so rapidly that her mother had the impression that she flew over them.

But if Catherine did that already at five, before the vision of Jesus and the three apostles above the Dominican church, with how much greater reason must she have done it afterward, as her desire to enter the Order grew more and more definite and she felt the need to confer with her confessor.

For she had only him to whom she could speak about it, or to her childhood friend Thomas della Fonte.

EARLY PENITENTIAL PRACTICES

Does that mean that her mother, who cherished Catherine above all her other children, was aware of nothing—the disciplines she was taking, alone or with her companions, the fasts and abstinences she was imposing on herself, the long silences she observed, and her numerous visits to the convent of the Dominicans?

Lapa was too shrewd and curious not to be aware of all that and not to suffer because of it. But what especially exasperated her, because she saw in it a permanent obstacle to her desire to see Catherine married at some future date, was Catherine's neglect of her appearance and lack of interest in her beauty.

By the time Catherine reached the age of twelve, Lapa redoubled her demands that Catherine give her body more care. Raymond of Capua relates that she taught Catherine to wash her face more often, to arrange and adorn her hair, and to occupy herself with all that concerns a woman's beauty, so that she might more readily attract those who would be tempted to ask for her hand.

At that time neither Catherine's mother nor her brothers and sisters suspected that she had taken a vow of virginity. On seeing her so preoccupied with devotions and penances, Lapa very likely considered it nothing more than the caprice of a young girl, due to some crisis in her physical growth or perhaps a crisis of conscience. She had heard of the vision of Fontebranda six years before, but probably had not attached much importance to it, or perhaps she remembered it so well that she was haunted by the idea of seeing to it that her little Catherine would be married in two or three years.

Seeing that her counsels came to nothing and that Catherine remained more interested in the appearance of her soul than that of her body, Lapa formed an alliance with her eldest daughter Bonaventura in order to put an end to Catherine's resistance and, if possible, to change the direction of her thoughts. At the urging and example of Bonaventura, whom Catherine dearly loved but who, like Lapa, highly esteemed the things of this world without being disinterested in those of the next world, Catherine consented to take better care of herself. Nevertheless, in the depths of her heart she remained firmly resolved never to marry. Her choice had been made at the age of five; she had chosen Jesus Christ for her spouse and would have no other.

We know from her confessors that Catherine was unwavering on this point. We even think that she yielded so much the more easily to the pleadings and example of Bonaventura to devote a little more care to her appearance because in doing this she had no intention of pleasing men. She herself later admitted this to Blessed Raymond, who questioned her on the subject and was uneasy at seeing her exaggerate her remorse for the pecadillos of her youth. Her only intention at the time had been to please her sister whom she especially loved. But it was precisely that for which she reproached herself, for she had for an instant, as she said, preferred her sister to God. Out of affection for her, she had done what for love of God she would never have done. When later we analyze Catherine's concept of the love of God and when we establish to what degree she lived it, we shall better understand the struggle of conscience and the nuances of feeling which agitated the soul of the twelve-year-old child.

The consciences of the saints had needs which extend far

beyond the dark zone of the sins which are classified as mortal or venial and even beyond the luminous area of the evangelical counsels. Their love of God is so pure, so disinterested, so absolute that even a legitimate affection such as fraternal love appears to them as a fault, if it inspires in them actions that are little in harmony with their love of God. Such was Catherine's attitude in regard to the attention given her bodily appearance and the concessions made to the tyranny of fashion.

Raymond of Capua, who heard Catherine's confession when she was in the full flowering of her spirituality and possessed a doctrine of life that was very certain and very rich, declares that in his opinion Catherine not only had never committed a mortal sin, but he had found her so free of venial sins that most of the time he could not discover any offenses in her daily confessions. Nevertheless Catherine, who was in no sense scrupulous, did not cease to weep until the time of her death for the sins of vanity caused by her exaggerated affection for her sister Bonaventura during her twelfth year, although never had the idea occurred to her at that period to try to please anyone in particular or to renounce her vow of virginity. In this characteristic trait of her early adolescence, we recognize the whole Catherine. At the sight of her remorse for having even unwittingly dared to balance for an instant the love she owed to God against that which she felt for her sister, we can imagine what she will become one day when she will love God with her whole heart, her whole soul, and all her strength and will subordinate everything in her life to such a love. Her personal life will be interiorly transformed by it and at the same time her apostolic life will be greatly increased.

Then she will love her neighbor as herself for the love of God. Her love will be so explosive, so to speak, that it will ignite the fire of charity in the souls of all those, sinners or not, who have the good fortune to come in contact with her.

But we should not anticipate. Let us rather return to the time when Bonaventura finally persuaded her little sister to be more solicitous about her appearance. At that time, Raymond observes, the fervor of Catherine's prayers and meditations was somewhat lessened. How long did this last? It is quite difficult to say precisely, but according to Raymond it seems to have lasted until the death of Bonaventura in 1362. Catherine was then about fifteen. The unexpected death of her older sister came like a thunderbolt and immediately put an end to the double life that Catherine had been leading for some time, prompted on the one hand by her affection for her family and on the other, by the imperious demands of her vocation. The latter prevailed.

Once again herself, Catherine resumed her penitential practices with renewed vigor and again satisfied her need for solitude. She devoted herself so much the more to bodily mortifications because she felt she should expiate her sins and pray for the repose of the soul of her sister who had deliberately urged her in the path of vanity only because she was ignorant of Catherine's vow of virginity and, like their mother Lapa, thought only of seeing that Catherine would be married.

Although Bonaventura was not a saint, as some have claimed, neither was she a wicked woman, as others would have us believe. Let us remember that she could not tolerate that her husband and his friends should indulge in vulgar or indecent conversations in her home. Such conduct made her physically sick. But like the Sienese of her day and, indeed, like many women of all times, she thought it possible to follow the dictates of style and fashion without sacrificing anything of her duty as a Christian wife. Moreover, we know that in the fourteenth century, even in a town as Catholic as Siena, laxity of morals in certain worldly circles went hand in hand with a lively faith. A Christian woman like Bonaventura needed a strong character to safeguard her morals while yielding to the dictates of fashion in the manner of dress. Then as today, in order to create, preserve, or augment their beauty, women used various cosmetics, tinted and arranged their hair, and took great pains to adorn themselves with valuable ornaments of gold and jewels. Christian as her family certainly was, Bonaventura had probably never gone beyond the moral bounds, but within these limits she had not scrupled to follow the world and to compel Catherine to do it also. When Bonaventura died, her little sister had no rest until she had obtained her salvation from God's mercy. To this end she multiplied her prayers and increased her penances until she had been heard.

TESTING THE VOCATION

Once assured by God of the eternal salvation of her sister, Catherine again dedicated all her time and care to the religious life. The idea of a Dominican vocation, which she had allowed to remain dormant during recent years, revived suddenly and was more intense and more appealing than ever. If it had depended on Catherine alone, she would have carried it out immediately. But Lapa was getting old and she felt that her daughter, who was now fifteen, had reached a marriageable age. They would find a husband for her without delay. Placed between God's call to the religious life and the strong determination of her mother to see her married, Catherine felt herself torn asunder. The more she increased her prayers and mortifications, the more intractable and obstinate her mother became. It is remarkable that in this tragic duel which involved her eternal destiny more than her temporal future, Catherine never for an instant lost her calm and composure nor did she deviate from the respect she owed her mother. The more Lapa wept, the more silent Catherine became. The sarcasm, impatience, and anger of the mother were met with silence, limitless patience, and an infinite sweetness. Nevertheless, it had to end in one way or another. It was now a question of the interest of all and of the peace of the family.

Since Catherine did not know what to do and Lapa, on the contrary, remained firm in her decision, each sought counsel of a Dominican friar. Raymond does not name him, but it is not difficult to identify him. None other than Thomas della Fonte, always the friend of the Benincasa family, seems indicated. Perhaps that is why the *Miracoli* does not hesitate to name him; nor is tradition mistaken in this. On the one hand, Thomas della Fonte knew Lapa well; on the other hand, he had the complete confidence of Catherine. He knew that the former would forego the marriage of her daughter only if the project were to become impossible, and he knew Catherine well enough to realize that her resolution to remain a virgin in accordance with her vow was inflexible. Consequently, he advised Catherine to take the only step that would, temporarily at least, safeguard her vow and thwart the plans of Lapa: that of cutting her hair. The advice was good, and Catherine did not have to be told a second time. She returned to her room and let down her blond hair, of which her mother was so proud and which Bonaventura had perhaps taught her to bleach, or at least to braid and decorate. Taking scissors in hand, she proceeded to cut the beautiful tresses, and when the act was done, she covered her head with a veil. Then, fortified by prayer and penance, she awaited the foreseen or unforeseen consequences that this act would inevitably entail.

All the documents agree, with slight variations, on the incident we have just related. Did Catherine cut her hair herself, as Raymond states, or did someone help her? Did she later deliberately take off her veil in her mother's presence or did Lapa, suspecting the truth when she saw this famous veil, tear it off by force? It makes little difference. The important thing for anyone who wishes to know the depths of Catherine's soul is to know how she conducted herself toward her parents at this turning point in her life, when they heaped insults upon her for her coup d'état and set out to make her life at home inconceivably miserable. All the witnesses consulted by her biographers concur in acknowledging that Catherine had never manifested greater serenity, more joyous abandonment to the will of God, or greater respect and obedience to her family. Never had her self-control, founded at the same time on her love of God, her vow of virginity and her inflexible fidelity to the spouse of her choice, Jesus Christ, shown itself stronger, nor her judgment more sound. It was a sort of miracle that she succeeded in reconciling the demands of God's will with those of her family on this delicate point on which the two wills were obstinately opposed. In the end, by reason of her patience, she successfully resolved those dissonances into a perfect harmony.

We shall now show how Catherine accomplished this, recounting the incidents that followed Lapa's fury at the sight of the shorn head of her daughter. In so doing we shall better understand how God, in permitting this family drama, wished to make Catherine aware of her Dominican vocation and at the same time to prepare her for a profound interior life that no external thing would ever disturb and for an apostolic life whose breadth and originality would astonish only those who are ignorant of the divine heights in which it had its source.

As soon as Lapa noticed that Catherine no longer had her hair—the beautiful hair which she had taught her to care for—she flew into a violent rage and voiced insults and threats.

"Ah! so this is the way it is," she said to her. "Well, it's all in vain, my girl. Your hair will grow in, and though your heart should break, you will marry." Catherine's brothers and sisters, who had long carried a grudge against her because of her secret life, on hearing the cries uttered by their mother, rushed into the room where the scene was taking place and added their own insults to those of Lapa. Raymond tells us that even Catherine's father, normally of a gentle disposition, could not restrain his anger. Without losing her calm, Catherine let the storm pass, put her veil back on her head, and silently returned to her room.

Then began a pitiless war against Catherine which her patience would one day bring to an end. Her mother attacked her on her most sensitive points. She knew that Catherine above all loved her room, because there she had freedom of her thoughts, her feelings, and her actions in her communications with God. Lapa deprived her of her room and forced her to share the room of her young brother, Stephen, although Catherine's mother was not unaware of the fact that she spent her free moments in penance and prayer. The maid was dismissed and Catherine was commanded to perform the tedious domestic work. As Raymond observes, they heaped upon her all the outrages, insults, and contempt that are ordinarily most painful to a woman's heart.

But none of these things troubled Catherine. Under the inspiration of the Holy Spirit, she formed in her heart a hidden interior cell which she resolved never to abandon for any external affair whatsoever. This interior cell was a substitute for her own room and in addition to this, she was not hindered from continuing her nightly vigils and her penances in the room she shared with Stephen, when he was deep in slumber. Then, under the inspiration of the same Holy Spirit, she mentally transformed the paternal home into that of the Holy Family of Nazareth. Our Lord was represented by her father; the Virgin Mary, by her mother; the apostles and disciples, by her brothers and sisters. Then it was no effort for her to answer their insults and contempt with an obedience and devotion which at first astonished them, and then made them admire her. Far from complaining about them, she anticipated their desires, so to speak, and obeyed them with a joy that flooded her countenance with radiance.

However, the day came when God Himself intervened directly to stop this long and cunning warfare. It was the day when Catherine's father unexpectedly entered the room of Stephen to get something he needed and surprised his daughter kneeling in a corner and rapt in prayer. A small dove, white as snow, hovered over the head of Catherine. When James entered, Raymond tells us, the dove spread its wings and seemed to escape through the window. When questioned by her father, Catherine had been unaware of the presence and flight of the dove. Astonished, James went out, pondering all these things in his heart, until the day in the near future when he gave his daughter back her complete freedom.

LA MANTELLATA

In the meantime, Catherine, who was gradually maturing through these trials which forced her to live more within herself, face to face with God in her interior cell, felt herself recapturing the desire to enter the Dominican Order. She had never really abandoned the idea which had grown in her since her childhood, but the events that we have faithfully reported (in the order in which they seem to have occurred) had distracted her attention from it. She was not unaware that if God, whom she loved with all her heart and who, she knew, rewards a hundredfold, had tested her to this extent and had detached her so severely from the world and even from her own family, it was for the purpose of attaching her more closely to Himself, so that being occupied only in loving Him, she could do so with complete freedom. She would make Him known and loved by those around her as circumstances, which are humble messengers of the divine will, would require. It was in that precisely that the Dominican vocation consisted.

It is not surprising that her desire to enter the Order of Friars Preachers should be revived at that time and take deeper root. If we believe Raymond, the most sympathetic and discerning of her confessors and the one from whom Catherine had never hidden any of the main events of her life, it was also the time that God chose to enlighten her about her vocation and to reveal to her His plans. He sent St. Dominic to her, who appeared holding in his hands the habit of the Sisters of Penance and said to her: "My dearest daughter, take courage and fear no obstacle, for you will certainly be clothed in this habit which you desire."

That same day, consoled and strengthened by this vision which was closely related to that of the apparition of Jesus and the apostles above the church of the Dominicans, Catherine assembled her family and gave a small speech which we can summarize as follows: "It is time that you know the truth of this matter. If I have so vehemently opposed the proposed marriage that you have planned for me, it is not through childishness or caprice; it is because it was impossible for me to act otherwise. Eight years ago I made a vow of virginity and I chose Jesus Christ as my Spouse. Now more than ever I am determined to remain faithful to this vow and to this choice. The very stones would more easily be softened than would my heart be deflected from this holy resolve. Therefore, it is useless to continue a struggle that can never be settled. Nothing, nobody, will prevent me from doing the will of God. Ask me to be your servant; I am quite willing to serve you joyfully. Or drive me from the house and my Spouse, Jesus Christ, who must be obeyed first, will take care of me and will not suffer me to fail in anything."

We can imagine the amazement of Catherine's parents and of her brothers and sisters on learning from Catherine's own lips that she was bound by a vow and on seeing that she was resolved to remain faithful to it at any cost. They loved her too much not to be moved and they burst into sobs. In addition, now that they knew the will of God in her regard, they were too good as Christians to put any obstacles in her way. At first they did not know what to answer, but Catherine's father, who had seen the dove over her head during prayer and knew many other extraordinary things that he had kept in his heart, spoke up in the midst of the general emotion and answered his daughter: "Fulfill your vow freely and do what the Holy Ghost will inspire you to do." Then, turning toward the rest of the family, he spoke with all his authority as head of the household: "From now on let no one dare to molest this child. Let her serve her Spouse freely and pray for us."

The grandeur and simplicity of this family scene recall the beautiful days of primitive Christianity, when young virgins, whose parents or persecutors tried to force them into marriage, did not hesitate to die rather than betray the vow they had secretly made to belong only to Jesus Christ. In that instant the roles in the Benincasa family were reversed. By the forcefulness of her speech and the power of her intrepid will, which no conceivable human power could ever withstand, Catherine subjected all minds to herself and conquered all their hearts. The slave of Jesus Christ regained all her freedom in order to serve Him better. She asked and obtained a room for herself alone, where she could pray and do penance at her good pleasure.

This is not the place to discuss in detail the austerities to which she gave herself for the sole purpose of proving to God her love for Him and to expiate her sins. We shall merely note at this point that in order to enter into the spirit of her Dominican vocation and to imitate St. Dominic to the best of her ability (for she already considered himself his daughter and had taken him as a model), she took the discipline three times a day with an iron chain, the first time for herself, the second for the living, and the third for the dead. However, such penitential practices did not prevent her from being gay and from always presenting a serene countenance to those around her. In this she resembled St. Dominic, if one can believe the account of Blessed Cecilia who, with a sure and luminous touch, has left us such a vivid portrait of him that one has the impression of hearing him speak and of seeing him. Besides, did not Catherine herself say of the Order of St. Dominic that it is all broad, all joyous, all perfumed, and a true garden of delights?

However, the reader will not have difficulty in believing that after all the moral trials she had endured and the frightening routine of austerities to which she submitted herself, Catherine suffered a breakdown of health. It weakened her for the rest of her days. Lapa, even when she railed against her daughter and made her life difficult, had never ceased to love her, although in too human a manner. She deeply grieved to see Catherine wasting away. She tried to make her daughter give up her penances, her fasts, her abstinences, her vigils, and her disciplines, but she did not succeed. Then the idea occurred to her to take Catherine to a sulphur bath not far from Siena, hoping in this way to cure her and at the same time to distract her mind. The only result was, as Raymond tells us, that in the midst of the delights of the bath, Catherine found a new way of afflicting her body—by letting herself be burned by boiling water as it gushed forth from the pipes.

Shortly after their return to Siena, as a consequence of the physical and moral trials which she had endured, Catherine fell gravely ill. She was afflicted with a rash which covered her whole body with blisters and eruptions and she was consumed with a burning fever. Catherine did not fail to recognize any advantage that might further her plans and, like divine Providence, she knew how to draw good from evil. Consequently, she took advantage of this illness and the pity it inspired in her mother to obtain a favor she desired above all else—that of entering the Sisters of the Third Order of Penance of St. Dominic, called in Siena by the expressive name of *Mantellate,* because of the large black mantle they wore over their white habit.

As we have explained elsewhere, the Brothers and Sisters of Penance sprang from the Dominican Order as a branch from a trunk filled with life. Wherever a convent of friars was established, friends of the Order, both men and women, inspired by their spirit, nourished by their teachings, and edified by their example, endeavored to live according to the Dominican spirit and to promote the Dominican apostolate. The name of Third Order was given to societies of men and women who, under the spiritual direction of the Fathers, wished in their own way and in the degree possible to them to share the religious and apostolic life of the Dominican Order.

The First Order is made up of the preaching friars, while the nuns, who lead a life of prayer and penance behind the cloister grille, comprise the Second Order. By asking to enter the Third Order at Siena, where the *Mantellate* publicly wore the habit of the Order and consecrated themselves to the apostolate under the direction of a religious of the Sienese convent, Catherine was satisfying her desire to be a Dominican, to belong to the Order founded by the holy Patriarch Dominic, and to be counted among his daughters. There is no more reason to see any opposition between the First Order and the Second and Third Orders than there is to see any opposition between branches which spring from the same trunk. The same sap nourishes all and makes them bear, in greater or less abundance, the same fruits of life.

Once before, after the family scene previously described, Catherine had made tentative inquiries to be admitted to the *Mantellate*. She met with a refusal. Doubtless, no more at Siena than elsewhere, young girls were not excluded from the Third Order, but they were received with great hesitation and after a thorough investigation, especially if they were gracious and beautiful. It was feared that, even under the mantle of St. Dominic, their beauty might be a snare by which the evil one would attempt to make them fall.

But this first refusal did not disarm Catherine. When she was afflicted with the skin eruption which we have mentioned, she thought that the occasion was opportune for her to be proposed again as a candidate and she begged her mother to take pity on her. "If you do not obtain this favor for me," she told her, "I will die." Lapa, who did not like the

Mantellate but who, on the other hand, passionately loved her little Catherine and feared to lose her, hastened to plead with the Sisters and by virtue of her insistence she persuaded two of them to visit Catherine. Fortunately, Catherine's illness had so marred her beauty that the Sisters were not aware of any special danger on that score, but what did strike them was the beauty of her soul, her love of God, the purity of her affections and morals, her simplicity of manners, and her incomparable humility. They left Catherine's room completely captivated by this chosen soul and they had no difficulty in seeing that she was accepted as a candidate. The Sisters first obtained the consent of the Brothers, as Raymond reports, and then at meeting of the Sisters themselves they voted unanimously for Catherine's admission. Within a few days Catherine had recovered her health, cured more by the joy she felt at this good news than by medical remedies.

Not long after, Catherine received the habit of St. Dominic from the hands of Father Bartholomew Mantucci, director of the Third Order, in the Chapel of the *Mantellate* which was annexed to the church of the Friars Preachers, above which the first vision had appeared to Catherine nine or ten years earlier. According to more authentic calculations and taking into account the scattered information found in contemporary writings concerning Catherine, it seems that the clothing occurred in 1363, only a year after the death of her elder sister. Indeed, Bonaventura must have rejoiced in heaven, which she had entered partly through the prayers and penances of Catherine, and she must have been happy that she had failed to make Catherine prefer the style of the day to the white tunic and full black mantle of the Sisters of Penance.

Scarcely had she become a *Mantellata* and been clothed

with the Dominican habit than Catherine resolved once more to change her manner of life in order to adapt it better to the demands of her vocation. As a true daughter of St. Dominic, she not only cultivated in herself his apostolic spirit, but she used the very means instituted by the holy Patriarch to labor effectively for the salvation of souls. Like the friars, she prayed in the day and at night. Her penances substituted for the monastic observances and even surpassed them in number and severity. As for sacred study, which St. Dominic had first introduced as an instrument of religious and apostolic sanctification, Catherine accomplished much in her own way. She did not follow courses of philosophy or theology because she could not read or write, but she did even better. She imbibed all her sacred doctrine at its very source, in contemplation and under direct dictation from God. Her personal experience did the rest. Later we shall explain Catherine's doctrine and we shall show how she first applied it to her own life for her personal sanctification and then passed it on to the countless souls whose salvation God had entrusted to her.

CHAPTER 2 ✍

Siena and Avignon

TO appreciate the significance and quality of Catherine's apostolate it is necessary to have a clear understanding of the milieu in which she labored and of the sources which nourished her apostolate. This second chapter is devoted to a study of the environment in which Catherine lived, struggled, and grew to maturity. The two following chapters will contain an analysis of the authentic sources of her prodigious apostolate. Only then shall we be able to understand how this humble daughter of St. Dominic, completely imbued with the same spirit of faith and driven by the same irresistible fire of charity as was the founder of the Order of Preachers, spent herself for the salvation of souls, using the same means chosen by St. Dominic but, like him, adapting them to her time and environment.

We do not intend to talk in generalities about Siena, Italy, or the Church in the time of St. Catherine. Other writers with much more authority and skill than ours have said all that it is necessary to know. Presuming the reader's knowledge of general history, we shall highlight the significant moral, political, social, and religious conditions at the second half of the fourteenth century, to which the apostolate of Catherine ran counter. If these difficulties are viewed from the aspect of charity as Catherine viewed them in order to resolve them, they will help us to perceive, beneath the complexity, the profound unity of her apostolic method, which was impregnated with the spirit of faith and burning charity.

SIENA

Of all the towns of Italy which have been ravaged by men and time in the course of that country's history, perhaps Siena has best preserved its medieval aspect. Seen from a distance, perched on the rock from which it surveys a broad horizon of wooded hills cut by deep ravines, Siena reminds the passer-by of the countrysides of Botticelli or Perugino. Inside the city the impression is no less striking. Siena is ever a city of the Middle Ages, less austere than Florence, more friendly, and less affected by modern life. Its inhabitants, gifted with a native good humor, speak the purest Italian in the whole peninsula.

Certain sections of Siena, such as the cathedral and its environs and the public square, which forms a half-amphitheater intended for the *Palio,* have preserved their ancient physiognomy. Here and there one discovers little crossroads and completely isolated corners that are reminiscent of the Orient. The Church of St. Dominic, with its famous frescoes by Sodoma, rises from the end of a verdant terrain where neighborhood chickens run free and donkeys bask in the warm sunshine. From this elevation, as from an acropolis, the eye follows the undulating blue crests of the Etruscan hills as they press on like waves as far as Perugia and Orvieto, Valterra and Florence.

There is a soul in the charming body of the old town, an undying memory which takes the living back to days of long ago. An angelic vision seems to hover in the gentle Sienese sky and St. Catherine is still its queen.

What is the essential difference between the Siena that

spreads out before our eyes and the fourteenth-century Siena that Catherine knew? Although much remains of that epoch—the cathedral, the Church of St. Dominic, several beautiful palaces, a few towers, two or three beautiful fountains, among them, Fontebranda—one no longer sees the beautiful ensemble of towers which rose above the more important homes and from a distance gave the town the appearance of a cluster of reeds.

But what of life in present-day Siena as compared to that in the time of Catherine? Apart from several ancient customs which still survive and provide an exciting or picturesque touch in the peaceful existence of the old city, nothing remains except fragments of the archives to recall the wealth of the twelfth century when the rich Sienese merchants had vanquished their competitors by force and ruled the town wisely, sharing their prosperity with their fellow-citizens. Nor does anything remain of the political life of the sixteenth-century when feuds and rivalries triumphed over wisdom and bred incessant civil wars. Although, strictly speaking, Catherine had never been involved in politics, it is impossible to understand the astonishing political aspect of her apostolate unless she can be seen against the agitated and impassioned background of her day. True, this age was but the natural result of a long historical evolution in which the Sienese, now merchants, now soldiers, began gradually to sacrifice the common good for class interests and their own personal gain.

What were the various factors that cause this evolution? We shall attempt to enumerate them, without writing a history of Siena or going into great detail. But we must recall the essential facts, for without them the temporal and local aspects of Catherine's apostolate cannot be clearly understood.

Siena reached the zenith of its wealth and glory toward the middle of the thirteenth century. From the beginning, its commercial history had been intimately linked with its political history. The Sienese were merchants, and in addition to the sale of cloth, which was made in Siena on a large scale, they formed caravans to transport to France and England and other foreign countries the spices of the Orient which they had purchased in Venice. But their renown and fame as bankers even surpassed their reputation as merchants. Their clever handling of money, so that they could make it yield a hundred to one, was proverbial. Even during the days when their position as Ghibellines and friends of the Emperor Frederick made them suspect to the Guelphs and to the Roman Curia, they remained the bankers of the Holy See. This would seem to prove that if money has no odor, as the popular saying goes, neither does it have any political preferences.

Nevertheless, the Sienese merchants and bankers, who toward the end of the thirteenth century were to make Siena one of the most important cities of Europe—much greater than London or even Paris—had to wage a gigantic struggle both against the feudal lords who taxed the caravans which passed through their domains and against their rival in business, the city of Florence. They set themselves to this two-fold task with stubbornness, skill, and marvelous *sang-froid,* proving themselves good soldiers as well as incomparable merchants. The struggle was long and bitter, marked by astonishing successes and serious reverses, until the famous victory of Monteaperti in 1260 broke the power of Florence.

Siena could then throw off the secular yoke of the feudal lords and press its own upon the surrounding cities that had long been exploited. Instead of laying aside their arms, the merchants formed an alliance with the emperor and

took over the government of the republic. Among the committees of all kinds that functioned in Siena at that time,
that of the Twenty-Four, whose members were recruited
from all classes, evolved rapidly into a stable magistracy of
definite political caliber, for it was composed exclusively of
Ghibellines. The people struggled constantly to make this
committee the sovereign authority in the State. Soon their
powers were so extended that the Twenty-Four could control all other committees that had any right or authority to
be involved in the affairs of the city.

Siena at that time knew great glory. Well protected by her
soldiers and well governed by her officials, her merchants,
while seeking to further their personal and class interests,
did not forget those of the city. They wanted Siena to be
great and powerful and rich in public institutions. During
the regime of the Twenty-Four, the University of Siena appeared for the first time as a completely organized municipal
institution. The Cathedral was begun in 1245 with money
provided by the State. The number of hospitals increased
and their management improved. And all during this period
the generosity of the State kept pace with the generosity of
individual wealthy citizens. Thus the aristocracy of money
left its imprint on the city. Next to the ancient, somber, and
fortress-like palaces of the nobles, rose the splendid dwell-
ings of the rich merchants or bourgeois. It seemed that those
happy times, depicted in a fresco by Lorenzetti in the Hall
of Peace in the Communal Palace, would last forever.

Unfortunately, the Sienese, though gifted with a rare
degree of business acumen, did not possess an equal degree
of political skill. On the morning after the battle of Monteaperti, the wine of victory went to their heads. Instead of
profiting by their victory in Tuscany to re-establish friendly
relations with the Guelphs, the triumphant Ghibellines

thought only of humiliating them. Some even spoke of raz-
ing Florence, which was then the center of the Guelph party.
So violent was the spirit of retaliation that Rome grew
alarmed. Pope Alexander IV excommunicated the Ghibellines, even though they were the bankers of the Roman
Curia, and Urban IV withdraw his patronage and completely released their debtors from all obligations.

At a distance of seven centuries, one may be tempted to
smile at the notion of a Pope's resort to a spiritual weapon
against the merchants, who were interested only in temporal
things. However, in that century of faith the authority of
the Pope was still unshaken and excommunication was the
surest and most effective method of bringing the Ghibellines
to their senses and of making them lay down their arms. As
a matter of fact, the merchants were rendered powerless to
regain their influence and the commercial disintegration
which followed was one of the causes which eventually
brought on the political decadence of Siena. The Twenty-
Four tried hard to fight against the Pope and against the
feudal lords, but the defeat of the Ghibellines at Benevent,
the death of their ally Manfred, the hanging of Corradino,
grandson of Frederick, and the beheading of their own chief
Provenzano Salvani on June 11, 1269, hastened the collapse
of their interests. The committee of Twenty-Four became
so unpopular that it was forced to yield its power to a council of thirty-six members recruited from among the Guelphs
who had been recalled from exile.

The powerful merchants then gained the ascendancy by
subordinating politics to business, for they deserted the
cause of the Ghibellines to rally to that of the Guelphs. The
situation, which was already critical, grew worse, for from
that moment a party spirit impregnated the government of
the Sienese republic and led to the despoliation of power

and participation in government by any class other than that of the merchants. In 1280 the Council was reduced to fifteen members, and in 1285, to nine. From then on, class warfare was in full swing. "Italy," says Geoffrey Fenton, in his version of the Sienese history of Anselm Salimbeni and Angelico Montanini, "is a nest of factions par excellence and the market place of the tumults and troubles of the world."

Nowhere in the peninsula did the madness of these factions cause more harm to the State than in Siena. Forcibly excluded from any participation in public affairs, many nobles spent their time settling family quarrels, while others went to swell the ranks of the mercenary troops that were then beginning to pounce upon unfortunate Italy. Destitute of military leaders, the bourgeois gave more and more attention to the accumulation of wealth. The warlike spirit died out among them. Incapable of leading a campaign, they lost sight of their obligation to uphold the prestige of the State. They desired only one thing: peace, peace at any price.

In 1328 a great famine, accompanied by its cortege of crimes and epidemics, devastated all Italy. People pillaged the shops and came knocking at the gates of the Palace of the Signory to ask for bread. The Nine answered this appeal by hanging several rioters but did little to lighten the sufferings of the poor. Siena needed an extraordinary vitality to withstand all these afflictions: civil wars, bankruptcy, and famine. Twenty years later, in 1348, the plague came to give the final blow to the government of the Nine who, because of the partisan spirit they fostered and the cruel methods they used to subdue their adversaries, were mainly responsible for the violences that had reddened the city with blood. At the same time, the government of the Nine had made Siena a sumptuous city where luxury and corruption flourished.

Party government had never been popular in Siena. The plague of 1348, which in a few months had caused more than two-thirds of the city to perish, thoroughly shook governmental authority. This was due mainly to the lack of organization it caused in public services, the disorders which naturally followed such a catastrophe, and the commercial insolvency which followed in its wake. A coalition of nobles and the people, supported by the Emperor Charles V, finally overthrew the government.

The Nine were succeeded by the Twelve, who, on September 2, 1368, were likewise rejected by the nobles and replaced by at least four distinct partisan governments during the last four months of the same year. Finally, a purely democratic council, formed from the common people, yielded to the Reformers, who very wisely tried to establish a more enduring government by admitting four members of the Twelve and three members of the Nine.

But, as one writer has remarked, the political maladies from which the republic suffered were incurable. Even the cloisters were more or less affected by it. On all sides there was nothing but dissensions, quarrels to the death, and revolts. The better citizens exhausted their energies in family vendettas or in party wars.

We find an echo of all these disturbances not only in the chronicles of the times, where the authors, according to their party allegiance, charged their enemies with the blackest crimes, but also in the *Assempri* or *Examples* of a Sienese hermit of the fourteenth century, Fra Philip Agazzari, and especially in the letters of St. Catherine of Siena. For it is in the midst of all the afflictions of these troubled times and under these partisan governments that St. Catherine lived and exercised her apostolate.

However, it is not enough to sketch the political condi-

tions of Siena at the time of Catherine in order to understand the immediate milieu which served as the field of her
apostolate. For she did not have to struggle only against the
political customs of her day, first in Siena and then throughout all Italy, in order to destroy the partisan spirit and re-
establish peace; she also had to fight against a great laxity in
morals. This moral decadence was partially caused by the
political atmosphere of violence and class egoism, but even
more so by the spirit of the Renaissance and a movement of
unbridled individualism which, toward the middle of the
fourteenth century, sought to release people from all con-
straints of the moral and religious order, even the most
sacred. True, a century before, the communes had undertaken to shake off the yoke of feudalism and to substitute
a more humane rule for the tyranny of the feudal lords. But
it is a serious error to confound, as too many historians do,
the spirit of freedom which at the dawn of the thirteenth
century contributed to the liberation of the communes, with
the pagan spirit which inspired the leaders of the Renaissance and gradually won the masses. In the case of the communes, it was only a question of freeing a certain number of
individuals from an external servitude which for centuries
had been a violation of the rights of the human person. In
the case of the Renaissance, it was the human person himself that the liberal attempted to free from every restraint,
including religious and moral laws, as if man's freedom consisted essentially in the right to live in absolute independence of everything and everybody, with neither faith nor
law.

There is an abyss between these two concepts. The first
aimed only to break the feudal chains in order to assure the
exercise of human liberty to each individual. The second, on
the contrary, planned to substitute for human liberty ruled

by reason, a liberty which mocks reason and recognizes no law of thought and action other than instinct and individual passions.

In spite of all the good that can be said of the literary Renaissance which began in Italy with Petrarch and Boccacio toward the middle of the fourteenth century and later filled libraries and museums with masterpieces, it is regrettable that from its very beginning it was more or less consciously infected with a pagan Renaissance which has rather done a work of death in souls. It is true that the modern world dates from this period, but that is not a point in favor of the pagan Renaissance whose deathly germs have had time to develop since then and little by little have spiritually devastated all Christian peoples.

What characterizes the modern world, as it has evolved before our eyes, is an almost complete ignorance of traditional moral values on the part of the masses and an absolute contempt for those values on the part of the elite and those who flatter themselves as leaders. Amidst the accumulated ruins of the moral world there remains today only brute force to resolve the conflicts of sentiments and interests that break out between nations or between fellow citizens of the same nation. The right of might has suppressed all other rights. More than that, all the marvels invented for the well-being of man by that science which would one day replace morality and religion are now in the process of turning against man. Men hate one another today with all the vehemence and ardor with which they ought to love one another. The power which they have at their disposal incites them to kill one another and to destroy a world civilization which has been painfully and laboriously established. This is the way they use their marvelous inventions when a true sentiment of human and divine brotherhood would have prompted them long ago to use these things in a manner that would assure a better life to the greatest number, a life more worthy of the human person.

The primacy of might has swept away all those things that uphold the honor of man and maintain a certain equilibrium among nations—personal conscience, the dignity of the human person, respect for the family and authority, regard for the rights of others, an awareness of the brotherhood of man, and Christian charity. Once reason and faith are contemned and the salutary restraints which duty imposes on right are destroyed, then a lawless urge to enjoy oneself prevails over everything else. From here it is only a step to violence, which terminates in bloodshed; always, of course, in the name of freedom.

In the time of St. Catherine, when the pagan breath of the Renaissance began to poison the consciences of man, or at least to deaden them, there took place in Siena in a small way what is happening today on a large scale. In the atmosphere of violence which was created by party factions, a great number of people, especially those who had the means, avidly sought amusements and pleasures as a means of escape or a compensation for so many evils.

The Sienese have always shown a childlike enthusiasm for festivals and amusements. In the second half of the thirteenth century, when the city was overflowing with wealth, neither the suffering caused by famine and the plague nor internal dissensions could suppress the high spirits of the people. They gave themselves energetically to their favorite games and sports—sham battles, hand-ball, horse races, or the *Palio*. The *Palio* was almost as ancient as Siena itself and was part of the celebration in honor of the Assumption, which was always the most popular feast for the Sienese. The common people also had their games and contests on the square of the Signory, and they were especially fond of a game called *Pallone,* the forerunner of football. They conducted their festivities with less ceremony than the aristocrats and with more rudeness or even brutality.

The pleasure of the hunt and of the table went hand in hand. Luxury was especially manifested in the clothing and perhaps at Siena more than elsewhere women readily submitted to the slavery of fashion. In Catherine's time, women's tastes had reached a passion for blatant attire. One needs but read the *Assempri* of Fra Philip Agazzari to be convinced. Without sparing the usurers, the impenitent gamblers, the blasphemers, the worldly religious, and the wayward priest, he reserves the best and most biting of his sarcasm for women whose cheeks are rouged or whose dresses are so tight that one of them died at table in the middle of the banquet on her wedding night. But, like Catherine and, a little later, Bernardine of Siena, Philip lays special blame on those Christian women who are both coquettish and pious; who have two faces, "that of God" and "that of the devil." We have already seen that Bonaventura, the elder sister of Catherine, although pious and honest, sacrificed to the goddess of fashion and tried to draw her little sister in her perfumed wake.

Such was the society of Siena in Catherine's day; rather, such was one of the aspects of this society. For if, as Fra Philip said, the devil exerted his influence, God also had His faithful followers. In those days one was not struck as one is in our day by the graciousness of these people who are the most refined, the most civilized, the most artistic, and speak the most musical language in all Italy. The Sienese went to extremes and lacked moderation. They relished contrasts.

In Catherine's time Siena was the most turbulent city

in Italy and the seat of discord and agitation; but it was also a city of saints and merited the title "Vestibule of Paradise." Among the inhabitants was Blessed Bernard Tolomei, the founder of the Congregation of Monte Oliveto; John Colombini, a rich merchant who, after having held the highest positions in the State, abandoned all to preach the gospel to the poor and founded the Confraternity of the *Poveri Gesuati,* the cavaliers of Christ; Blessed Peter Petroni, the Carthusian; and Fra Philip, the author of the *Assempri.* Lastly, it was in Siena that Bernardine grew to manhood. In the following century he would be the greatest preacher in Italy.

To read Catherine's letters to her fellow townsmen without understanding fourteenth-century Siena is to run the risk of not grasping the profound inspiration, the peace and charity, and the apostolic method she used to touch the depths of the hearts of her correspondents. Moreover, it is necessary to extend this description somewhat and to say a few words about the spiritual ravages which descended not only on Siena, but on Rome, Florence, Pisa, Genoa, Naples, and all Italy as a result of the Pope's departure from Rome for Avignon.

AVIGNON

Avignon was the residence of the papacy from 1308 to 1377. Catherine of Siena, who died in 1380 at the age of thirty-three, had ample time to ascertain everywhere, both in Italy and within the Church, the deplorable results of the popes' departure from Rome and their long sojourn at Avignon. She often made allusion to this in her letters and even in the *Dialogue,* but she always places the situation in a supernatural light in order to judge whether it was a question of political events or simply a state of morality.

From this point of view, her judgments are severe but impartial. On the other hand, the historians and chroniclers of her time, depending on whether they were adversaries or partisans of the papacy, exaggerated in one direction or the other, blackening the popes or whitewashing them beyond due measure.

Catherine did not enter into politics. On the contrary, she denounced the intrusion of politics into the domain of religion. Her good common sense, as well as the intuitions of her enlightened and burning charity, enabled her to show that the greater part of the evils that afflicted her country and the Church were due to the mixture of politics with religion and that it was useless to search elsewhere for the causes of the civil or foreign wars and the general decadence of morals. She says and writes as much to the popes, the heads of rival factions, prelates, religious, priests, laymen, and to all those who would be tempted to subordinate religious to political interests, instead of subordinating politics to religion. She says it to all who forget that God ought to be served first and that when this is done, all the rest will follow its normal course and there will be tranquillity of mind and of heart.

Meanwhile, disorder reigned everywhere, primarily in Italy but also in the entire Church. After May 7, 1312, that is to say, after the entrance into the peninsula of Henry VII, King of the Romans, the whole country was in a perpetual state of revolution. Rome itself was nothing but a battlefield where the Guelphs and Ghibellines indulged in bloody assaults. Under Clement VI (1342–1352) the inevitable war set Italy on fire and the flames did not subside until the sword of Albornoz had reduced to impotency the various tyrants, both great and small, who harrassed the peace of the peninsula.

Pope Urban V (1362–1370) believed the time had come to re-establish the papacy at Rome, but his efforts came to naught. In 1370, he was at Montefiascone, but with incredible inconsistency the Romans, who wanted to keep him within their walls, forced him out by uniting with the Perugians, who had revolted against the Church and had joined forces with the mercenary troops who for some time had been ravaging the country. Florence in its turn raised the standard of revolt against the papacy and drew in its revolutionary wake not only its own citizens, but also the subjects of neighboring states, under pretext of remedying the abuse committed by the legates of Pope Gregory XI, whom Catherine would persuade to return to Rome in 1377.

Such was the political milieu in which Catherine of Siena had to struggle and she struggled to exhaustion in order to try to restore peace, with no other motive than to save the souls of those whom political madness had blinded, and with no other method than that inspired by her charity under the two-fold enlightenment of her faith and her remarkable common sense.

But that is not all. While factions were tearing Italy apart, the infidels were threatening the Church. Willingly or unwillingly, a Crusade had to be organized against them. That was the dominant thought of the popes of this period, even the popes of Avignon, from Clement V to Gregory XI. But how could a crusade be organized when Italy was utterly ravaged by internal war and France was at war with England? Before all else, these two enemy nations must be reconciled. A voluminous diplomatic correspondence proves that on this particular point the popes used all their influence. But their most persevering efforts collided with the ill will of the French and English courts.

The idea of a Crusade against the infidels also haunted the

mind of St. Catherine. She loved the Church too deeply to be indifferent to the external danger which threatened it, and the thought that an invasion by the infidels would be fatal to thousands of Christian souls, inspired her to write to Gregory XI, urging him to organize the Crusade at any cost.[1]

Meanwhile, the Church itself needed a reform from within, especially the clergy which, on the one hand, had been blinded by political ambition and, on the other hand, had been infected by the individualistic spirit fostered by the Renaissance. Historians and chroniclers have concealed none of the internal evils from which the Church suffered under this double influence, as much in Italy as at the court of Avignon. Better informed as we are today, thanks to an abundance of documents which they did not have at their disposal, we are in a position to compare their testimony and to make allowance for exaggerations prompted by party feeling.

Nevertheless, the fact remains that on all sides, in the cloister as well as among the diocesan clergy, at the court of Avignon as well as in the most humble diocese, the spirit of dissension and a renascent paganism exercised their nefarious influence. For example, as regards the Dominican Order, the publication of the Acts of Chapters of the Roman Province from 1243 to 1344 reveals the degree to which political feelings had penetrated into the convents, where Guelphs and Ghibellines had their partisans and their adversaries. Such conditions did not facilitate conventual life, especially the practice of fraternal charity and obedience. The Chapters threatened with excommunication and even with imprisonment those religious who would meddle with politics or would appeal to outside influences in order

[1] Letter 238.

to exert pressure on their superiors or ignore their commands. It is easy to see how in this overheated atmosphere, passion often gained the mastery over virtue and a certain laxity of morals gradually succeeded the primitive fervor. Although even in these troubled times holy religious were not lacking, nevertheless, mediocre religious abounded. In the time of Catherine of Siena and Raymond of Capua it will be urgently necessary to impose a reform and it will not be too difficult for these two great souls to introduce it into the Order and to assure its success.

In the *Dialogue,* Catherine gives us a very detailed picture of the disorder that party politics and pagan individualism had caused throughout the entire ecclesiastical hierarchy. Nevertheless, to be just and truthful, it must not be forgotten that before speaking of bad pastors, Catherine, under the inspiration of God, had praised the good pastors who, faithful to their priestly vocation, had served and were still serving God in charity and justice. We would refer to the *Dialogue* all those who are desirous of knowing the details of this picture.[2] There they will see with what frankness the saints knew how to uncover the wounds of the soul, not for the unwholesome pleasure of exposing them to the full light of day, but to apply more efficaciously the red-hot iron of penance. We shall here cite a passage from the *Dialogue* in which Catherine virgorously denounces the "fever of money" which then raged in the Church and provoked all sorts of shameful evils. This passage is characteristic of her objective and impartial manner of approaching these delicate problems, without any political passion but as an apostle interested only in the salvation of souls.

"For thou seest that those who desire prelacies and

[2] Cf. *The Dialogue of St. Catherine of Siena,* (tr. Algar Thorold, Burns Oates & Washbourne: 1925), pp. 247–95.

benefices in the holy Church buy them with many presents, offering whatever commodities or moneys they happen to possess. And that the wretched sellers do not consider whether the buyer is good or evil, but out of complaisance and love of the gift which they have received, strive to place this putrid plant in the garden of the holy Church. To this end these wretches will give a good account of him to the Christ on earth, so that both of them use falseness and cheating toward the Christ on earth on a point on which they should approach him with the whole simple truth. But if the vicar of My Son should perceive their sins, he ought to punish them, and from the one take away his dignity if he do not amend his evil life. As for the other who buys, it would be well that he should be sent to prison as his part of the bargain, so that he may be corrected for his sin, and that others may take warning and be afraid, so that no one else may imitate him. If the Christ on earth do this, he does his duty, and if he does not, his sin will not be unpunished when he has to give an account before Me of his flock.

"Believe Me, My daughter, today this is not done, and it is on this account that My Church has fallen into such sins and abominations. They do not seek to know or try to investigate the good or evil life of those to whom they give prelacies. And if they do seek at all to find out, they ask questions of those who are as bad as themselves and who give nothing but good testimony, because they themselves have similar defects and think of nothing else except dignity of position, and gentility and riches and polished conversation. Worse than all, it will sometimes be alleged as a motive to the Consistory that the person in question is beautiful. What devilish doings! They should seek the ornament and beauty of virtue, but they look rather at the beauty of the body. They should seek poor and humble

persons who avoid prelacies in their humility, and they
choose those who seek them in vanity and inflated pride.

"They admire knowledge. Knowledge in itself is good
and perfect when a learned person is also good, honorable,
and humble in life. But if knowledge be joined with a
proud, dishonorable, and wicked life, it is a poison. . . .
See then that science, good in itself, is not so in him who
does not use it aright; it rather lights for him a penal fire if
he will not amend his life. They should therefore rather
seek out men of good and holy life than learned men who
live evilly, but they do the contrary. Those who, besides
being good and virtuous, are great in learning, they despise
as fools, and the poor they avoid, because they have nothing
wherewith to pay them. See, therefore, that in My house,
which ought to be a house of prayer and where the pearl
of justice ought to shine, together with the light of learning, honor, and holiness, and the odor of truth, lies
abound." [3]

What Catherine puts into the very mouth of God about
the laxness of the morals of the clergy of her day, she repeats
without wearying in her letters to Gregory XI and Urban
VI and to cardinals, bishops, prelates, princes, and officials
of the cities of Bologna and Florence. Her apostolic heart
is revolted by the thought that souls are lost through the
fault of those very ones who have the duty of saving them.
We need only the testimony of this "soul of fire" to form an
idea of the evils of all kinds that afflicted her country and
the Church.

However, Catherine's testimony is in full accord with
what other documents report of the history of her times.
But her testimony has this one great advantage over others:
it was not inspired by political ambition or flattery. Cath-

[3] Cf. *The Dialogue,* chap. CXXVII, pp. 267 ff.

erine, we repeat, had nothing to do with politics. She posed as neither a statesman nor a diplomat. Certainly, she was not unaware of the political philosophies that divided her country and tore the seamless robe of the Church. On certain occasions she even displayed an innate sense of diplomacy, not the kind that resorted to deceit, but the kind that was inspired by charity in the service of truth. Her sincere love of God and souls, joined to that delicacy of spirit which she possessed to a high degree and which sometimes appeared under the form of naiveté, made up for all the artifices of purely human diplomacy, whose whole art consists in giving to a lie the appearance of truth.

A final trial, the most cruel, had been reserved for Cathtrine two years before her death—the Great Western Schism. After having done all that she could to help Gregory XI leave Avignon for Rome, Catherine had the sorrow of seeing this saintly Pontiff die on March 27, 1378. Ten days later, the sixteen cardinals present in Rome assembled in conclave and, as early as the following morning, elected as pope the Archbishop of Bari, Bartholomew Prignano, who took the name of Urban VI. When the six cardinals of Avignon were officially informed of the election, they acknowledged and congratulated the Pope chosen by their colleagues. The Roman cardinals informed the head of the Empire and the other Catholic sovereigns. Cardinal Robert of Geneva, the future Clement VIII of Avignon, sent a letter in the same vein to the King of France, his relative, and to the Count of Flanders. Peter de Luna of Aragon, the future Benedict XIII, wrote the same news to several Spanish bishops. In a word, on the morning after the election of Urban VI, nobody contested its validity. But on September 20, 1378, at Fondi, thirteen of the Roman Cardinals who had elected Urban VI and even before the

election had formally manifested their intention of elect-
ing a lawful pope, who had enthroned him at the Vatican
Palace (then St. John Lateran), and who, on April 18, had
solemnly crowned him at St. Peter's, entered into conclave
and elected Robert of Geneva as pope. Robert took the
name of Clement VII and went to establish himself at
Avignon.

What could have happened that was serious enough to
justify such an about-face? Were these cardinals convinced
that in spite of their intention to elect a lawful pope, as they
had stated at the Roman conclave, the election had been
invalid? By no means. They had simply realized that Urban
VI, their first choice, did not measure up to the hopes they
had placed in him; that he had a brusque, violent, suspi-
cious, and even extravagant temperament, with no regard
for anyone not of his opinion, even if it were a cardinal of
the Holy Church. Doubtless, that did not suffice to make his
election invalid, but it was enough to make him unbearable
and to cause his electors to lose their heads. The result was
the Great Western Schism.

Catherine of Siena took the only part that her charity
and her wisdom inspired her to take. While there was still
time, she had had the supernatural courage to warn Urban
VI, to urge him to use more moderation and gentleness,
and to appeal to his charity. But her efforts were without
success. Neither was she afraid to censure the conduct of the
rebellious cardinals toward the Pontiff they had previously
and legitimately elected.

At the end of the *via crucis* with which her apostolate had
begun more than fifteen years before, the Western Schism
was truly the Calvary on which she was crucified, like her
divine Master Jesus Christ, and where she died of sorrow
at seeing the Church involved for so long a time in a ter-

rible crisis. The Church would ultimately survive, but at the price of a multitude of souls incapable of withstanding such a scandal without spiritual harm.

Certainly much more could be said about the fourteenth-century political, moral, social, and religious milieu in which Catherine lived and exercised her apostolate. But enough has been said to enable the reader to realize many of the difficulties that she had the courage to face and that her charity most often surmounted in a manner that was peculiarly her own. We shall determine the transcendency and efficacy of her method when we discuss the divine sources of her teaching and her contemplation and the luminous and fruitful character of her charity. For St. Catherine, as for the Church, there is only one charity, which consists in loving God for Himself and, in virtue of this love of God, obliges us both theoretically and practically to love our neighbor as ourselves. Catherine will go so far as to say that the love of the neighbor thus understood is at once the experimental proof and the measure of our love of God.

CHAPTER 3

Spiritual Doctrine

IN his history of Siena, considered one of the best and most penetrating, Langton Douglas dedicates an entire chapter to St. Catherine of Siena and concludes by saying that St. Catherine seems to him to be the most attractive character of the fourteenth century and that no Sienese, except perhaps Aeneas Sylvius Piccolomini, played a greater role in history. In an evaluation of Catherine he states that it is easy to find matter for criticism in this woman. She was credulous, subject to hysteria, and she made immoderate use of the discipline, which only aroused the emotions she tried to bridle and aggravated, rather than remedied, the evils she proposed to cure. She did not realize that without health of body, complete health of mind is impossible. But health, temperance, and moderation were not characteristic of the Middle Ages. He finally asserts that we ought not wrong St. Catherine for going to excess in her practice of virtue, for it is to the heart rather than to the intellect that great religions appeal. A great religious prophet must necessarily agitate; hence, for him love must always remain the most important thing in the world. It would be folly to wish that David, St. John, St. Francis, or St. Catherine had not been what they were.

There is something good and something bad in this opinion. The facts oblige this honest historian to bow before Catherine as "the most attractive character of the four-teenth century," one of those who, according to him, has played the greatest role in history. But because he is igno-rant of the real sources from which Catherine drew the necessary light and energy for the accomplishment of her heroic deeds, he reproaches her—as do others—although with a nuance of regret and sympathy, for having been credulous, for having given herself immoderately to corpo-ral penance, and for having neglected her health in her intense interest in the life of the spirit. Doubtless, he recognized that it is necessary to search her heart for the secret of her life and her activity, and that love held the first place in both. But what kind of love? He does not know. If he is aware that it is the love of God, he does not under-stand that in the saints such a love makes terrible demands which explain their asceticism, their mysticism, and their apostolate.

We cannot understand the mysteries of Jesus—His birth, His sufferings, His death—unless we put ourselves in the full heart of God, a God of love who so loved men that to satisfy for their sins and to help them gain their salvation, He gave them His only Son. Likewise, it is in the "full heart" of St. Catherine that her life must be considered—its entirety and its details, its unity and its harmonious diversity.

We cannot ask a historian to put himself on that super-natural plane in order to write the life of St. Catherine or, if the life is already written, to criticize its sources. But what are we to think of a historian who, under the pretext that there is too much of the supernatural in a saint's life—too many miracles, ecstasies, and visions—would accuse biographers of fraudulently including supernatural phenomena in order to procure more certainly the canonization of their heroine and would then tax his ingenuity to arrange or derange the facts, to change dates, to substitute a completely new chronology for one already established by numerous irreproachable witnesses? A historical reconstruction of this kind is more difficult to justify than the supernatural which it attempts to eliminate. Undoubtedly that is why other historians of scientific probity leave to the specialists—the psychologists, the theologians, and the Church—the task of interpreting facts whose historic exactitude is not on trial, but whose supernatural context clearly escapes the competence of the historians.

Finally, the method of evaluating the life and activity of Catherine of Siena from a purely human point of view, without denying the supernatural but abstracting from it, is scarcely of more value. To presume to explain her whole apostolate, or even certain aspects of her apostolate by making her the equivalent of a politician, a polished diplomat, or a great statesman (the greatest of her century, as has been said), is to understand nothing of her apostolic method nor of the supernatural motives that inspired her.

Humanly speaking, Catherine did not lack the qualities requisite for adapting her apostolate to the ideas and the political needs of her time. She could have filled the role of a polished diplomat or a brilliant statesman. She was highly gifted naturally, but she was still more gifted supernaturally. The originality of her genius and of her method was her ability to fuse harmoniously all her gifts, both natural and supernatural, in the fire of her love of God, without destroying any of those gifts. This charity explains everything in her, both her interior and her exterior life.

It gives to her asceticism, to her mysticism, and to her apostolate, that unity amid diversity which causes astonishment
and admiration in all those who seriously examine her life
in the light of her teaching.

SOURCES OF HER DOCTRINE

According to her own admission, Catherine of Siena did
not know how to read or write. Yet her admirable doctrine,
full of light and life, is to be found in her voluminous correspondence and especially in her *Dialogue,* which is regarded
as the spiritual testament of her life and which she dictated
to her secretaries during her ecstasies.

Who were her secretaries? Raymond of Capua has preserved their names for us, at least the names of those who
were the principal witnesses on whom he depended in com-
piling his list: Barduccio Canigiani, Stephen Maconi, and
Neri Landoccio. Speaking of Neri, at the end of the first
chapter in the third part of the *Legenda,* Raymond says:
"He was, with Stephen and Barduccio, one of the secretaries
to whom Catherine dictated her letters and her book. He
became attached to the spouse of Christ before the others,
leaving his father, who was still living, and his relatives in
order to follow her."

"It is for these witnesses and not for myself," remarks
Raymond humbly, "that I ask credence. They are more
worthy of it than I, for I know that they have imitated the
actions of Catherine more perfectly and as a result, they have
understood them better."

To their testimony is added that of Catherine herself, who
is above all suspicion. For if Raymond was not an eye-
witness to the incidents of which he speaks here, he learned
them, not only from the mouths of the spiritual sons of
Catherine whose testimony he guarantees according to the

sanctity of their lives, but also from the letters of Catherine herself, who often wrote to him at this period to tell him what was happening.

All these witnesses agree in acknowledging that they wrote the *Dialogue* from the dictation of Catherine during her ecstasies. Maconi, who later became a Carthusian, states in a famous letter that the entire *Dialogue* was composed by St. Catherine under the inspiration of the Holy Ghost. This is the source of our information. The teaching of Catherine, interspersed throughout her letters and synthesized in the *Dialogue,* has a supernatural origin. She learned it directly from God Himself and transmitted it directly to her disciples.[1]

However, in reading her letters and the *Dialogue,* one has the impression that although it may be divine in its origin, Catherine's teaching is marvelously adapted to the nature of her intellect. Like a prism of pure crystal through which light is refracted to form the beautiful colors of the rainbow, so through Catherine's intellect the doctrine which emanates from God reflects all the feminine nuances of her thinking. From one end to the other her teaching bears the mark of her spirit.

[1] Bartholomew Dominici declares in his deposition at the *Process of Venice* that some persons maintained that the religious instructed Catherine in her doctrine, when in truth she was their teacher. Gradually, through daily experience, everyone recognized that her learning was inspired by God Himself, both in her letters and in her *Dialogue,* which she always dictated during her ecstasies. He had seen her dictate different material to two secretaries at the same time. Sometimes she employed as many as three secretaries, not stopping between thinking and dictating as people ordinarily do. Her words flowed with her thoughts, under the same interior inspiration, as from a continual fountain. In the papal bull, *Misericordias Domini,* Pius II declares: "Her doctrine was infused, not acquired. She appears as a master before being a pupil."

In its substance and basic principles, though not in its manner of presentation, the teaching of St. Catherine is remarkably similar to that of St. Thomas Aquinas. Toward the close of his life, St. Thomas confessed to one of his disciples and confidants that he had learned more at the foot of the crucifix than in books. We know, also, that in drawing up the *Summa Theologica,* when he found himself grappling with a particularly difficult problem, he first had recourse to prayer. Divine assistance was not lacking to him in the course of his career as professor and writer, although he did not compose the *Summa* under the dictation of God as Catherine did her *Dialogue.* But whatever can be credited to the inspiration of the Holy Ghost in the doctrine of St. Thomas, it is certain that his teaching bears the human stamp of his genius. Everywhere in his writings is to be found evidence of that virile intellect, at once profound and lucid, which approaches a question, exhausts it, and leaves nothing in the shadow.

St. Thomas is before all else a speculative thinker who, in the question of principles, acknowledges the role of intuition but, when departing from the principles of reason or faith in philosophy and theology, deduces conclusions with the aid of reasoning. His method is essentially deductive. In each question that he studies before tying it in with other questions to make a synthesis, he proceeds slowly, step by step and article by article, until he has completely investigated the problem that has been proposed. As a result, his work gives evidence of a perfect balance between strong thought which is sure of itself and a perfectly adapted intellectual method. The divine and the human, faith and reason, mutually support and illumine each other without confusion or encroachment. The very words which St. Thomas uses to express his thought consistently give this impression of balance and power. They seem to burst forth from his speculative mind, translating all the nuances of that mind into words and images that are simple and transparent.

In the *Dialogue,* on the contrary, although the doctrine was revealed by God, Catherine reflects the nature and the needs of the feminine mind: more intuitive than speculative, more prone to suggest ideas through the use of well-chosen images than to draw conclusions by the process of reasoning. Moreover, here it is a question of a saint preoccupied especially in knowing God in order to love Him better and to love Him more in order to know Him better. In a word, it is a method more proper to contemplation than to speculation.

"What is unusual and marvelous," remarks Father Hurtaud in the preface to his French translation of the *Dialogue,* "is to see the mind of a humble girl, who had neither sacred nor profane learning, dedicated to the contemplation of eternal truth, the mystery of divinity, divine providence, love, and mercy, the abysses of iniquity and the splendors of grace, and with such ease and such penetration that one would say she was in her proper element, that her spirit frolics and plays in this light (to use one of her favorite comparisons) like a fish in water. We are astounded at the precise terminology, which theologians acquire only after long meditation and much effort, in which Catherine expresses simply and without hesitation but with certainty, without study but with exactitude, the highest wisdom and the most profound mysteries. How can one fail to be convinced that her learning is not from men when these sublimities, for which the scholars have prepared a technical vocabulary outside of which it would be dangerous, if not impossible, to express such exalted concepts, are now understood in the language of the people? Similarly, the eternal Word of the Father, disdaining royal pomp, clothed Himself in the form of a slave and chose to be born in a stable. By a new wonder, as the stable has now grown into a basilica, so the common speech, made sublime by the divine Word, has become, on the lips of this uneducated virgin and under the influence of the Holy Ghost, a choice language which in the formation of Italian literature rivals that of Petrarch in its purity, elegance, and richness. A powerful intellect becomes master of the forms of art by which it expresses itself and sublime thoughts make a sublime style. Here the intellect of this spouse of Christ is under the power of the wisdom of God."

Still more marvelous than the power of contemplation of this humble girl, the brilliance of her style, or the indescribable richness of her language, is the perfect equilibrium of her spirit, the mastery with which, in the doctrine of love which is revealed to her, she establishes harmony between love and knowledge.

After examining certain external manifestations of her intimate and personal life with God, such as the rigors of her asceticism or the multiplicity of her ecstasies, we would be tempted to think that this soul, whose heart burned with divine love and dreamed of setting the world of souls afire with the flames of her charity, valued only love and, provided it was intense and without limit, was not interested in regulating it or submitting it to the enlightened control of faith and prudence. Is it in this absolute sense that she understands the famous formula of St. Augustine: "Love and do what you will"?

Quite the contrary. If, with St. Paul, she makes charity the first of the virtues, she means, with St. Thomas, to submit the object of charity to the light of faith, and the exercise of charity to the control of prudence, that supernatural virtue of the practical intellect which she calls discretion or discernment. Nothing is more reasonable than her doctrine of love. Moreover, to judge correctly certain peculiarities of her ascetical and mystical life which shock our intellectual myopia and our moral mediocrity, they must be considered in the light of this doctrine. In spite of appearances, her life is not excessive. Inspired as it is by a love of God that is without limits, her love remains bathed in the light of faith and controlled, not by a human prudence without love, but by a supernatural and infused prudence that is strengthened by the gift of counsel which, in turn, measures the gift of self by the demands of true charity.

This we propose to demonstrate by drawing upon the doctrine of St. Catherine, and in particular those passages which especially show the harmonious blending of charity and faith and of faith and reason. They project such light on the interior life of Catherine and on her apostolate that when we have grasped them, we have captured the secret of her asceticism, her mystical life, and her extraordinary apostolate.

DOCTRINE OF LOVE

"Now, consider in the same way that the soul is a tree existing by love, and that it can live by nothing else than love, and that if this soul have not in very truth the divine love of perfect charity, she cannot produce fruit of life, but only of death." [2]

This perfect charity, which is a gift of God, can flower in the soul only on two conditions: the knowledge of God and the knowledge of self in God.

The knowledge of ourselves is the first fruit of a considera-

[2] *Dialogue,* Chap. X, p. 21.

tion of our spirit. "Open the eye of thy intellect," Catherine exhorts repeatedly in her letters. The natural insights of our intellect are useful and even necessary in a certain manner: they are gifts from God. "The soul I created in My image and likeness, giving her memory, intellect, and will. The intellect is the most noble part of the soul, and is moved by the affection, and nourishes it. And the hand of love, that is, the affection, fills the memory with the remembrance of Me and of the benefits received, which it does with care and gratitude; and so one power spurs on another and the soul is nourished in the life of grace." [3] "The soul that does not see into My Truth with the eye of her intellect, cannot hear or know My Truth. Wherefore, in order that thou mayest the better know it, rise above the feelings of thy senses. . . . Thou knowest, as I have told thee, that without the light, no one can walk in the truth; that is, without the light of reason, which light of reason you draw from Me, the true Light." [4]

This soul of fire loves the light, whatever may be its source. She praises the understanding that helps us to know ourselves and also the science by which we know things. "Science in itself is good," we read in the *Dialogue*. "Knowledge in itself is good and perfect when a learned person is also good, honorable, and humble in life. But if knowledge be joined with a proud, dishonorable, and wicked life, it is a poison." [5] St. Catherine, like St. Teresa, if she had to choose between two directors, one of which was a wise and experienced theologian and the other was a saint but lacked these necessary qualities, would undoubtedly have chosen the first. In any case, as Père Lemonnyer ingeniously remarks, "It is not she who would designate as privileged can-

[3] *Ibid.*, Chap. LI, p. 97.   [4] *Ibid.*, Chap. XCVIII, p. 190.
[5] *Ibid.*, Chap. CXXVII, p. 268.

didates for Christian sanctity the souls in whom imagination and feeling dominate." [6] That stands out in all her
writings.

Nevertheless, when it is a question of knowledge of God
and knowledge of self in God, Catherine declares without
equivocation that although these natural insights are proper
to us, they are not sufficient. In the picturesque style which
is typical of her, she insists that we should open the eye of
our intellect, which must be supernaturally enlarged by the
"pupil of faith." The pupil of this eye is a very holy faith,
whose light makes us "discern, know, and follow the way
and the doctrine of My Truth—the Word incarnate; and
without this pupil of faith she would not see, except as a
man who has the form of the eye but who has covered the
pupil (which causes the eye to see) with a cloth. So the pupil
of the intellect is faith, and if the soul has covered it with
the cloth of infidelity, drawn over it by self-love, she does
not see, but only has the form of the eye without the light,
because she has hidden it." [7]

Elsewhere again, in a letter to a Florentine lawyer, Ris-
toro Canigiani, she writes: "We have in us a natural light
which the Creator has given us to distinguish good from
evil, the perfect from the imperfect, the pure from the impure, light from darkness, the finite from the infinite. It is a
knowledge with which God has gifted our very nature. . . .
It is proper, then, that we should use this natural light . . .
and with it, look for the good wherever it is to be found.
In looking for it, we will find it in God. [8] . . . But to know
God well and to know ourselves in God—two indispensable
conditions of our charity—it is necessary that this natural

[6] A. Lemonnyer, O. P., *Notre vie spirituelle a l'école de sainte Catherine de Sienne*, pp. 23 ff.

[7] *Dialogue,* Chap. XLV, p. 84.   [8] Letter 301.

but imperfect light be joined to the supernatural perfect light which is infused into our souls with grace: [9] faith properly called, received at baptism.[10] Then we shall see the ineffable love that God showed us through the mediation of His Son, and which His Son manifested by shedding His Blood under the fire of love." [11]

Such is the portal of light through which it is necessary to pass in following St. Catherine in order to penetrate into the temple of love. We can love God only on the condition that we know Him and know ourselves in Him. But when the intellect, enlightened by faith, knows Him as He revealed Himself to us, the will is disposed to love Him and to answer love with love. So God commands us to love Him for Himself and to love, with the same love, our neighbor as ourselves for the sake of Him.

Perhaps it will be said that there is nothing new in this doctrine, that it is simply the gospel. But it would be disastrous if Catherine, who claimed to be instructed directly by God, were to change something in the teachings of the gospel and in the doctrine of the Church! What is astonishing is that a humble girl, who had never studied books or pursued theology courses, transmits to us a theological doctrine which is absolutely orthodox and which answers so well the demands of reason and of faith that it seems like a living echo of the doctrine of St. Thomas. What is new in the doctrine of St. Catherine (we shall have occasion to lay stress on this point in the following chapter) is that it is not the fruit of speculation, but of contemplation; it is a doctrine of life, breathing with love and personal experience. As we read in the *Dialogue:* "The soul cannot live without love, but always wants to love something, because she is

[9] *Ibid.*   [10] *Dialogue,* Chap. IV, p. 6.
[11] Letter 301.

made of love, and by love I created her. And therefore I told thee that the affection moved the intellect, saying, as it were, 'I will love, because the food on which I feed is love.' Then the intellect, feeling itself awakened by the affection, says, as it were, 'If thou wilt love, I will give thee that which thou canst love.' " [12]

All through the *Dialogue* God reveals to Catherine the existence, the nature, and the grandeur of this Being, by making Himself known to her in all the manifestations of His love for men and making her know herself in Him, both as to the dignity and the indignity of her being. The doctrine that God teaches Catherine in the *Dialogue* she assimilated so well and made so much a part of her language and her life that when we read her letters, where she addresses her correspondents directly, we have the impression that it is her own doctrine that she is teaching them and that she drew it from her own interior life. All her correspondence is permeated with it and in each letter, whether she writes to this one or that one, we find her personal touch, not only as to her style and inimitable language, brilliant with light and rich with color, but also this accent of authority, which would be astounding in a girl so humble and so conscious of her nothingness if we did not remember that she is speaking in the name of God. It is not really she who speaks, but God Himself who speaks through her, even when she dictates her letters to her disciples.

Let us try now to draw from the writings of Catherine that admirable doctrine of love as revealed by God and lived by her. Then and then only shall we be able to interpret her life. For the life of Catherine is her doctrine in action, drawn from the sources of an almost continual contemplation in the presence of God, where faith and charity, reinforcing

[12] *Dialogue,* Chap. LI, p. 97.

one another, produce, under the inspiration of the Holy Ghost, an abundance of supernatural intuitions which, in theological language, are called the acts of the gifts of the Holy Ghost and which are in the soul of a saint the permanent antennae of love.

"And know, My dearest daughter, that no one can escape from My hands, for I am who am, and you are not in yourselves, but only so far as you act through Me, who am the Creator of all things which share the gift of being, except sin, which is nothing, and therefore not made by Me. And inasmuch as it is not found in Me, it is not worthy of being loved. For this reason, the creature sins and offends, because she loves that which she ought not to love, namely sin, and hates Me, whom she is obliged and bound to love, because I am the supreme Good, and have given her being with such fire of love." [13]

In these few lines of the *Dialogue* we have the essential element of the divine teaching on creature love. In a letter from Cathine to Bernabo Visconti, her personal expression transposes an intellectual formula into mystical language: "What heart is so hard and stubborn that it would not melt at seeing the affection and love of divine goodness? Then love, love! Think! You were loved before you yourself loved because God, in the contemplation of Himself, is seized with love for the beauty of His creature. Moved by the fire of His love, He has no other aim but to give eternal life to His creature and to make him share in the infinite joy He feels in Himself. O inestimable love! What proofs You have given us of this love! [14]

It is properly the art of Catherine and of all great contemplatives to translate speculative truths into the language

[13] *Ibid.*, Chap. XVIII, p. 39.   [14] Letter 28.

of love and action and, by a sort of intuition of the heart, to
go straight to the reality that they express in an abstract
manner in order to live it concretely and impregnate all
their acts with it. At the burning contact of charity, the intellectual formulas which our mind naturally needs to express the highest truths and those most charged with significance—especially those which concern the nature of God
and our relations with Him as creatures—give place, under
the inspiration of the Holy Ghost, to the intuitions of the
heart. These direct glimpses of divine reality, which are
effected by the gifts of understanding, knowledge, and wisdom, enable the great lovers of God, the contemplatives, to
translate into the concrete language of words and images,
which spring from their minds like sparks from a hearth, all
that they have felt, experienced, or simply intuited concerning divine things. In reading the letters of St. Catherine we
receive the impression that the God of whom she speaks with
so much fire and in such luminous terms was not made
known to her through books and the teaching of men, but
in the school of reality and of experience. This impression
becomes stronger when we pass from the reading of her
letters to the record of her life.

HUMILITY AND TRUTH

Raymond of Capua tells us in the *Legenda* that our Savior
appeared to Catherine one day while she was praying and
said to her: "Do you know, My daughter, who you are and
who I am? If you have this twofold knowledge, you will be
happy. You are she who is not, I am He who is. If you keep
this truth in your heart, the enemy will never deceive you.
You will escape all his snares, you will never consent to do
any act contrary to My commandments, and you will ac-

quire without difficulty every grace, every truth, and every light."

"I am He who is, you are she who is not." This formula has nothing new in it; it is the one which God used in order to signify His presence to Moses in the midst of the burning bush. Since that time, the greatest theologians have commented on this statement and clarified it when they affirmed and demonstrated that in God there is no difference between His essence and His existence; that His essence is to exist; that He is through Himself, absolutely and infinitely, while we exist only through Him and depend on Him in all that we are or do.

It can easily be imagined how a metaphysician, juggling with the antithesis of being and non-being, becomes more or less vain by reason of the profound reflections that such a meditation inspires and the rich developments that it suggests. Quite otherwise is the attitude of Catherine. Once her mind has grasped the formula, "I am who am, you are she who is not," it penetrated her heart and passed into her very life. The verbal antithesis and metaphysical truth contained in the formula moved Catherine's heart. She not only had the idea, but she had a vital awareness that God is all and that she was nothing except in God. In the light of God, the infinitely supreme Being, she saw her own nothingness and recognized her total dependence on God. It was as if a strong hand were holding her above an abyss, and she was reassured only by the fact that this hand was that of a friend.

Catherine's humility, which orders her whole life in all its actions and from which charity itself draws nourishment, springs from no other source than this awareness of the infinite greatness of God and her own nothingness. God Himself undertook to instruct her in this regard: "No virtue,

My daughter, can have life in itself except through charity and humility, which is the foster-mother and nurse of charity. In self-knowledge, then, thou wilt humble thyself, seeing that in thyself thou dost not even exist; for thy very being, as thou wilt learn, is derived from Me, since I have loved both thee and others before you were in existence." [15]

This truth is the cornerstone of the temple of love, where Catherine's soul dwelt, and on which the whole edifice is supported. For if the humility that was in her soul as a result of the awareness of her own nothingness in comparison with God arouses and nourishes her charity, it also produces a horror of sin.

To see that in comparison with God we of ourselves are nothing, absolutely nothing, is normal. Far from being tragic, if this awareness of our own nothingness engenders humility, it is translated into actions of grace and charity as soon as one perceives that the love of God is the principle of all things. The tragedy begins only with sin, that is to say, with the deliberate attitude of a creature who knows that of himself he is nothing, that he is always dependent on God, that he owes all that he has and all that he is to God's love, and nevertheless reverses the roles, acting as if God were nothing and he, the creature, were everything.

Here again we have one of those antitheses in which a mind with sufficient penetration can play with words and ideas, while the conscience and the heart remain unmoved and one's spiritual attitude and conduct remain unchanged. But a soul as intelligent and fervent as Catherine's, which was made humble by the realization of her nothingness at the same time that her charity was inflamed, could not be brought to the concept of sin without being upset to the very depths of her being. In the entire *Dialogue,* with the

[15] *Dialogue,* Chap. IV, p. 6.

exception of the teachings on charity, there is no doctrine to which God more urgently drew the attention of His daughter and moved her heart, nor is there any to which she returns with more insistence in her letters.

"I have created man to My own image and likeness, in order that he might have eternal life and might partake of Me and taste My supreme and eternal sweetness and goodness. But after sin had closed heaven and bolted the doors of mercy, the soul of man produced thorns and prickly brambles and My creature found in himself rebellion against himself.

"And the flesh immediately began to war against the spirit and, losing the state of innocence, became a foul animal. And all created things rebelled against man, whereas they would have been obedient to him had he remained in the state in which I had placed him. By not remaining therein, he transgressed My obedience and merited eternal death in soul and body. And as soon as he had sinned, a tempestuous flood arose, which ever buffets him with its waves, bringing him weariness and trouble from himself, the devil, and the world. Everyone was drowned in the flood, because no one with his own justice alone could arrive at eternal life. And so, wishing to remedy your great evils, I have given you the Bridge of my Son in order that, passing across the flood, you may not be drowned, which flood is the tempestuous sea of this dark life." [16]

HATRED AND LOVE

We are now at the very heart of Catherine's doctrine, from which a light radiates to illumine the most obscure corners of her life. It is necessary to pause here for an instant if we

[16] *Ibid.,* Chap. XXI, p. 42.

are to discover the secret of her intimate relations with God in contemplation and her future apostolate among souls.

Hatred of sin and love of sinners: such are the two sentiments that God aroused in her soul when He revealed to her His loving solicitude for men. As profoundly penetrated with the recognition of her own nothingness as with the love of God who created her in His image and likeness, Catherine could not bear the thought that nothingness should seek to equate itself with being or that it should respond to love with hatred. The thought shocked and revolted her.

We have an admirable example of her reaction in the incident that took place after the death of her elder sister, Bonaventura. Catherine suddenly perceived that in order to please her, she had followed her advice and had busied herself more than was reasonable with her appearance, yielding to coquetry and fashion as her sister did. Where there had been apparently only an excessive and misunderstood sisterly affection, she saw a fault. She reproached herself for having preferred the affection of her sister to the love of God, for in order to please Bonaventura she had done something she would never have done if she were desirous of pleasing God alone. Raymond of Capua, to whom she later revealed these faults of her youth, considered it his duty to advise his readers that in his opinion there had not been even a venial sin.

But Catherine, who examined her conscience in the mirror of divine love, was not of this opinion. Convinced that of herself she was nothing and that God, who is all, had only drawn her out of nothing through His goodness, she ended by reproaching herself for not having sacrificed all of herself to Him and of not giving Him love for love, even in the smallest things. For years she tried to cleanse with her tears and voluntary penance what she called those sins of her youth, which had resulted from a lack of generosity toward God in a matter in which she had been prompted much more by sisterly affection than by vanity. Catherine was not the least bit scrupulous, but she was incredibly sensitive about the rights of God over His creature due to the fact that the creature of itself is nothing and owes God everything. All her life she had a horror of sin, especially any sin inspired by pride and self-love, which drives creatures to prefer the goods of this world to the sovereign good. We have only to read her correspondence to see that the horror of sin had almost become an obsession with her.

It was quite another matter once Catherine had a clear understanding of the price that God had paid for our sins in the person of the Word, His only Son, because of His love for sinners. When she understood that in spite of His hatred for sin, the Son of God had become incarnate and had resolved, in order to save sinners (on the condition, of course, that they consented to be saved), to shed the last drop of His Blood, she also began to love sinners with a love proportionate to the hatred that sin itself inspired. Two passages of the *Dialogue* enable us to understand the doctrine that inspired Catherine as a worthy daughter of St. Dominic and Christ to dedicate herself to the salvation of souls, and even to shed her blood to the last drop if God should ask it of her for the expiation of the sins of men.

"Thou seest His body all open on the wood of the Cross, pouring forth blood from every part, and that He has not redeemed you with gold or silver, but with His blood, through the greatness of His love. Not a part only of the world, but the whole human race, past, present, and to come, was contained in the satisfaction of that sacrifice.

And to none of you would the blood be administered, or the fire of divine love given, had he not first administered and given them." [17]

At another time Catherine addressed Jesus directly: "Sweet and immaculate Lamb. Thou wert dead when Thy side was opened. Why then didst Thou want to be struck and have Thy heart divided?" And the answer was given to her by God, as is recorded in her *Dialogue:* "Because My desire toward the human generation was ended and I had finished the actual work of bearing pain and torment, and yet I had not been able to show, by finite things, because My love was infinite, how much more love I had. I wished thee to see the secret of the heart, showing it to thee open, so that thou mightest see how much more I loved than I could show thee by finite pain." [18]

We can imagine that such a doctrine of love must have had some echo in the ardent soul of Catherine who, at the age of seven, only one year after her first vision above the Dominican church, had already made a vow never to have any spouse other than Jesus Christ. In spite of her precocious mind, she could not at that age foresee all that was involved in making such a vow. Several years later, when she understood definitely that the only way of proving her love for Jesus Christ was to collaborate with Him in the salvation of souls, she decided, in order to make this collaboration effective and fruitful, to enter the Order of St. Dominic and to consecrate her whole life to the apostolate. But it was only when Jesus chose her in turn for His spouse that her apostolic vocation acquired all its meaning and took on an exceptional amplitude.

From that intimate and solemn moment, Jesus and Cath-

[17] *Ibid.,* Chap. CXXVII, p. 265.   [18] *Ibid.,* Chap. LXXV, p. 139.

erine were one in heart and soul. Her biographers tell us
that an exchange of hearts actually took place. This means
that in espousing Jesus, Catherine espoused His motives
and His manner of living. As in Him, the love of God translated itself into an immense love of neighbor, and the way
that she took, in order to collaborate with Him in the salvation of souls, was the one He had traced under the inspiration of love: the way of the Cross. All her letters bear witness
to this intimate and loving union with the Crucified and
the doctrine which stands out is truly the message she addressed to mankind. Let us content ourselves with several
of the most significant extracts.

"The servant ought not walk in any other path than that
of the Master and the path of pleasure is not the path of the
Crucified. . . . Nothing ought to give us more joy than to
share in the humiliations and sufferings of Jesus. . . . Be
crucified with Christ crucified; follow Him on the road to
Calvary; become like Him and rejoice in opprobrium, sufferings, contempt, calumnies, and insults. Persevere to the
last in searching for comfort only in the Blood which streams
from the Cross. . . . Do not shrink when trials come, but
face them with a joyous countenance and accept them with
happiness. . . . Then bitterness will change into sweetness
and you will end your days sweetly resting on the Cross with
Christ crucified. . . . Just as the infant is nourished with
the milk of its mother, so the soul that loves God lives by
Christ crucified and walks constantly in His footsteps, following Him in the way of ignominy and desiring to rejoice
in nothing but sufferings and insults. . . . The soul clings
courageously to the wood of the Cross and contemplates it
with holy desire, seeing the burning and consuming Love
who shed His blood everywhere. Such a soul bears trials
patiently and, through love, renounces willingly all the con-

solations of the world. Persecution, torments, and pains become its best friends, for the soul has seen the Son of God
clothed thus when He could have chosen the most beautiful
vesture. . . . Clothe yourself, clothe yourself in Christ. He
is an armor so powerful that neither demons nor men can
strip you unless you consent. He is the supreme and eternal
sweetness that dissipates all bitterness. The soul that is thus
fortified and filled with Him considers as mire everything
that does not come from Christ. It wishes only to be like
Christ crucified, and thus rejoices in opprobrium and
calumnies." [19]

However, we must be careful to give the correct inter-
pretation to this doctrine on the imitation of Jesus crucified.
As we read in the *Dialogue*,[20] suffering is not an end in itself,
but a means. It is the means chosen by God Himself and
inspired by His supreme goodness to satisfy for our sins and
those of our neighbor. Confronted with the humanly invincible obstacle of sin, the creative love of God, far from
withdrawing, has rebounded with more violence and generosity. It devised the Incarnation and the Redemption.
Through love of sinners, the Son of God was made man to
suffer and die on the cross. Thus, all the penances that
Catherine practiced and recommended others to practice, in
order to supply what is wanting in the passion of Christ—
that is, our personal collaboration—were inspired by the
same love of God and souls. It is from love that they, like
those of Jesus, draw all their moral value and merits. Take
away this love, and suffering is not justified. It is then
neither an end nor even a means.

There is, then, nothing more like the gospel than St.
Catherine's doctrine of suffering in the service of love, and
nothing so orthodox as her teaching on the love of neighbor,

[19] Letter 39; cf. also letters, 73, 53, 26.   [20] *Dialogue,* Chap. XI.

considered as a corollary of the love we owe to God. To love God is to strive at the same time to love the neighbor that God loves. To love one's neighbor as oneself by suffering for him (and God has already given us the example in the person of Jesus) is one of the most authentic ways of proving our love of God.

"Love of her neighbor is developed out of love of Me, that is, out of that learning which the soul obtained by knowing herself and My goodness in her. When, therefore, she sees herself to be ineffably loved by Me, she loves every rational creature with the self-same love with which she sees herself to be loved. And for this reason the soul that knows Me immediately expands to the love of her neighbor, because she sees that I love that neighbor ineffably, and so, herself loves the object which she sees Me to have loved still more." [21]

GENEROSITY OF LOVE

But how can we prove to God that we love Him and that we love our neighbor? Hear the answer that God gave to Catherine: "If the soul elect to love Me, she should elect to endure pains for Me in whatever mode or circumstance I may send them to her. Patience cannot be proved in any other way than by suffering, and patience is united with love, as has been said. Therefore, bear yourselves with manly courage, for unless you do so, you will not prove yourselves to be spouses of My Truth, and faithful children, nor of the company of those who relish the taste of My honor and the salvation of souls." [22]

Is it necessary to add that this doctrine, so divine in its origin, so evangelical in its expression, is also, in spite of certain appearances, a very reasonable doctrine? One

[21] *Ibid.,* Chap. LXXXIX, p. 168.   [22] *Ibid.,* Chap. V, p. 10.

should, however, remember the words of St. Paul: "The wisdom of this world is foolishness with God." [23]

We have seen that certain historians and distinguished critics have sometimes reproached Catherine for her excessive penances, and in order to explain them, if not to justify them, have not hesitated to accuse her of hysteria. This is truly madness. One may as well reproach Christ because He chose Calvary to expiate our sins and to re-instate us in the grace of God. Moreover, the very men who reproach Catherine—and even Jesus—for having voluntarily sought out suffering, recognize that even from a human point of view the love of a mother for her child or the love of a citizen for his country inspire sacrifices that are analogous to those of the love of God. A mother, in order to save her son, or a patriot, in order to defend his country, find it necessary to impose heavy sacrifices on themselves and, if need be, to offer their lives. Why should that which is reasonable in the domain of human love cease to be so when it is a question of divine love? Is it less wise to sacrifice one's body for the salvation of the soul or for the soul of a neighbor than to have one's limb cut off to save the whole body or to give one's life to save one's country? There is no answer other than to deny God or admit the obligation of loving Him.

But if we put ourselves in the place of those who believe in God and who love Him, we must recognize that their love of suffering is only the logical manifestation of their love of God and of neighbor. There is no real love without the giving of self, and one does not give oneself without suffering. The degree of love and its disinterestedness regulate the quality and the intensity of voluntary suffering.

Fundamentally, suffering is the thermometer of love.

[23] Cf. I Cor. 3:19.

Thus, we can judge the infinite love of Christ for sinners by the enormity of His voluntary sufferings. Likewise, when it is a question of evaluating the sufferings of Catherine, we can do so only in the light of the love of God and of neighbor which inspired them. If the quality of such a love escapes the critics, let them say so; but even in holding only to the facts, they should at least acknowledge that between the voluntary sufferings of Catherine and her Christian charity there is an absolute bond. Her life and her doctrine are an unimpeachable testimony of it. To have recourse to hysteria in an attempt to explain the inexplicable is the last step that should be taken even from a purely human point of view, especially when it is a question of a woman as logical and balanced as Catherine. The luminous pages which she has written on the subject of penance show her good sense and psychological finesse, and in all charity we would wish to see it shared to the same degree by her detractors. We shall cite a passage from the *Dialogue* in support of this statement.

"These are the holy and sweet works which I seek from My servants; these are the proved interior virtues of the soul, as I have told thee. They do not consist only in those virtues which are exercised by means of the body, that is, with an external act, or with diverse and varied penances, which are the instruments of virtue. Works of penance performed alone without the above-mentioned virtues would please Me little. Often, indeed, if the soul perform not her penance with discretion, that is to say, if her affection be placed principally in the penance she has undertaken, her perfection will be impeded. She should rather place reliance on the affection of love, with a holy hatred of herself, accompanied by true humility and perfect patience, together with the other interior virtues of the soul, with hunger and desire for my honor and the salvation of souls. For these virtues demonstrate that the will is dead and continually slays its own sensuality through the affection of love of virtue. With this discretion, then, should the soul perform her penance, that is, she should place her principal affection in virtue rather than in penance itself. Penance should be but the means to increase virtue according to the needs of the individual and according to what the soul sees she can do in the measure of her own capacity. Otherwise, if the soul place her foundation on penance, she will contaminate her own perfection, because her penance will not be done in the light of knowledge of herself and of My goodness, with discretion. She will not seize hold of My truth and will neither love that which I love, nor hate that which I hate." [24]

It is from love, love of God and of neighbor, and not from exterior penances that Catherine's virtue and merit spring. Instructed directly by God, she repeats it unceasingly in her letters and in the counsels that she gives to her correspondents. Thus, it is according to her life, and not according to our prejudices, that we ought to judge her. Her life is filled with exterior penances which surpass in number and importance the penances practiced by the average Christian. But the same thing can be said of her virtues. Their heroic quality was proclaimed by the Church when she was raised to the altars. If there is a narrow line between her penances and her virtues, are we going to reproach her also for the heroism of her virtues? In a word, are we going to reproach her for having been a saint and, by the same token, the most brilliant figure of her century?

[24] *Dialogue,* Chap. IX, p. 19.

HOLY DISCRETION

The doctrine of St. Catherine of Siena is the best light we have at our command to clarify all the manifestations of her personal moral life and her apostolic life, especially those manifestations that at first jolt our prejudices or our egotism. In the final analysis, her love explains everything. But her love, whether it is a question of love of God, of self, or of neighbor, must be understood as she explains it in the *Dialogue* and in her letters, and not according to the restrictions or the deformations that our ignorance or our lack of comprehension would place upon it.

First, true charity, purified of all dross, presupposes a perfect knowledge of God and of one's self in God. Similarly, the practice of charity necessarily presupposes a special light, to which Catherine gives the lovely name of discretion and which is nothing other than the supernatural virtue of prudence. In the *Dialogue* God teaches His daughter that "true love knows well, because she carries with herself the light of holy discretion, that light which dissipates all darkness, takes away ignorance, and is the condiment of every instrument of virtue. Holy discretion is a prudence which cannot be cheated, a fortitude which canot be beaten, a perseverance from end to end, stretching from heaven to earth, that is, from knowledge of Me to knowledge of self and from love of Me to love of others." [25] Thus, under the influence of true charity, discretion regulates the acts of all the virtues. This is also the doctrine of St. Thomas.

We have already remarked that according to the doctrine of Catherine, charity, without being itself a light, can become a source of light. By means of the influence it exercises on the intellect which is illumined by faith, charity not only

[25] *Ibid.*, Chap. XI, p. 25.

puts us in a state to know ourselves better, but it enables us to regulate more efficiently the practice of all the virtues through the love we owe to God, ourselves, and our neighbor. That is properly the role of discretion and is the element that distinguishes it from all the other virtues.

Discretion, finally, is the art with which a soul, all vibrant with charity, realizes clearly all that it owes to God, to self, and to neighbor. Throughout the infinite and complicated web of the actions of each day's conduct the soul acts, not in a thoughtless and impulsive way, but with clearness, moderation, and complete self-control.

One of the first effects of discretion is to give the soul a sense of duty, a realization of what it owes to God, to self and to neighbor, and the practical manner in which it ought to fulfill all its duties in its daily conduct. In the *Dialogue* God clearly explains this doctrine to Catherine: "Dost thou know how these three virtues stand together? It is as if a circle were drawn on the surface of the earth, and a tree, with an off-shoot joined to its side, grew in the center of the circle. The tree is nourished in the earth contained in the diameter of the circle, for if the tree were out of the earth it would die and give no fruit. Now, consider in the same way, that the soul is a tree existing by love and that it can live by nothing else than love, and that if this soul have not in very truth the divine love of perfect charity, she cannot produce fruit of life, but only of death. It is necessary, then, that the root of this tree, that is, the affection of the soul, should grow in and issue from the circle of true self-knowledge which is contained in Me, who have neither beginning nor end, like the circumference of the circle, for turn as thou wilt within a circle, inasmuch as the circumference has neither end nor beginning, thou always remainest within it.

"This knowledge of thyself and of Me is found in the

earth of true humility, which is as wide as the diameter of the circle, that is, as the knowledge of self and of Me (for otherwise the circle would not be without end and beginning, but would have its beginning in knowledge of self and its end in confusion, if this knowledge were not contained in Me). Then the tree of love feeds itself on humility, bringing forth from its side the off-shoot of true discretion, in the way that I have already told thee, from the heart of the tree, that is, the affection of love which is in the soul, and the patience which proves that I am in the soul and the soul in Me. This tree then, so sweetly planted, produces fragrant blossoms of virtue possessing many scents of great variety, inasmuch as the soul renders fruit of grace and utility to her neighbor, according to the zeal of those who come to receive fruit from My servants. And to Me she renders the sweet odor of glory and praise to My name and thus fulfills the object of her creation.

"In this way, therefore, she reaches the term of her being, that is, Myself, her God, who am eternal life. And these fruits cannot be taken from her without her will, inasmuch as they are all flavored with discretion, because they are all united, as has been said above." [26]

It is evident that there is no question here of debts of justice properly so called, but of debts of love, which do not, of course, dispense with the debts of justice but far surpass them, for they are of another order. The question here is not the rights of man, but God's right to be loved for Himself and to be loved in us and in our neighbor. For we are in the supernatural domain of grace, where everything is gratuitious on God's part. It is not only a question of serving God—for which the virtue of religion naturally provides—but of loving Him and rendering Him love for love.

[26] *Ibid.,* Chap. X, p. 20.

The same thing is true in regard to our neighbor. It is not merely a question of being just toward him by respecting his natural or acquired rights but of giving him, for love of God, over and above that which is due him in justice, of loving him as ourselves by helping him to know and to love God by all the means at our disposal: prayer, teaching, counsels, almsgiving, sacrifices, and above all, good example. Discretion should enlighten us on all these points and show us what we ought to do or not do in regard to our neighbor. As God inspired Catherine to remark in the *Dialogue,* it forbids us to sin to help a soul to save itself. The remedy in this case would be worse than the evil. For we cannot flatter ourselves that we love God and at the same time hate Him—hate Him by sinning and love Him by substituting hatred for love in order to save a soul. "So thou seest how discreetly every soul who wishes for grace should pay her debts, that is, should love Me with an infinite love and without measure, but her neighbor with measure, with a restricted love, as I have said, not doing herself the injury of sin in order to be useful to others. This is St. Paul's counsel to thee when he says that charity ought to be concerned first with self, otherwise it will never be of perfect utility to others." [27]

In a magnificent letter to Sister Daniella d'Orvieto, Catherine returns to this doctrine of discretion and repeats what we have just said concerning our debts of love to God and our neighbor, but says it in a manner that is particularly suited to her and with a sense of moderation that shows her extraordinary psychological finesse. "The first rule that discretion gives to the soul consists in this: to render honor to God, good will to one's neighbor, and in regard to oneself, to hate sin and one's own sensuality. But

[27] *Ibid.,* Chap. XI, p. 25.

since the soul lives in the body, it is fitting that enlightened discretion impose a rule on the body also, for the soul uses it as a means to increase in virtue. . . . It imposes restraint on all the members of the body, so that they will be modest and temperate. Let the eye not look where it should not, . . . let the tongue avoid idle speech, . . . let the ear shun dissolute words. . . . To all, discretion gives a rule. And in order that the perverse law of the flesh, which fights against the spirit, may not throw the faculties into disorder, it imposes a rule upon the body. It mortifies it with vigils, fasts, and the other exercises that are all meant to put a rein upon our body.

"But note well that in all this, discretion sees only a means to grow in virtue, in due times and places and as need may dictate, and not an end which would push the soul to search out such and such a penance for its own sake. . . . If the body is too strong and rebels against the spirit, penance takes the rod of discipline, fasting, haircloth, long vigils, and places burdens on the body that it may be more subdued. But if the body is weak or has fallen into illness, the rule of discretion does not approve of such a method. Nay, not only should fasting be abandoned, but meat should be eaten and if once a day is not enough, then four times. If one cannot stand up, let him stay in his bed; if he cannot kneel, let him sit or lie down, as is necessary. That is what discretion demands." [28]

St. Catherine's teaching is identical in her letters and in the *Dialogue*. In reading the letters, one feels that she has profited personally from the divine lessons of the *Dialogue* and that to the authority of God she adds the authority of experience.

The virtue of discretion, or infused prudence, enlight-

[28] Letter 213.

ened by the inspirations of the gift of counsel, which removes all uncertainty and hesitation, is perhaps the distinctive trait of St. Catherine's spiritual physiognomy. "Her exterior life," observes Père Lemonnyer, "bears a profound and clear imprint. I think especially of that rare mixture of fearlessness in making plans and imperturbable assurance as to their execution, which reveals a soul that knows what it is doing and why. There is no trace of uncertainty as to the outcome, no hesitation regarding the means to be chosen. She gives the impression of a conscience that is sure of itself and a prudence that has control over all the threads of her actions. Doubtless, she was illumined by a special divine light, but this light she clearly appropriated to herself, incorporated in herself, and focused it on her interior virtues, so that under these miraculous illuminations it is she who controls the conduct of her life." [29]

In the preface of his *Saint Catherine of Siena,* Jorgensen makes a candid avowal on this subject: "To be sincere, I must confess that at first I felt less in sympathy with Catherine of Siena than with Francis of Assisi. In the energetic nature of the Sienese saint there is somewhat of a domineering spirit, an element of tyranny that was repugnant to me. Her perpetual and very feminine *Io voglio,* 'I will,' is in absolute contrast to the gentle Umbrian who preferred to see his lifework fail rather than make use of power and authority 'like the Podestà of this world.' . . . But gradually, as I began to know her more intimately, the same thing befell me that befell so many others during her earthly life —I was subjugated by her and had to acknowledge myself beaten." [30]

Jorgensen is mistaken when he attributes to Catherine an element of tyranny. He mistook her decisive spirit for

[29] A. Lemonnyer, O.P., *op. cit.,* p. 76.   [30] Jorgensen, *op. cit.,* p. V.

tyranny. She was too humble and too charitable to impose her ideas on anyone, although she had a clear view of the supernatural ends she was pursuing and a very certain judgment concerning the best means of attaining those ends. Under the force of her charity and in the perfect harmony of her will with that of God, she moved to action. "I will," she said, because such was the will of God. "I will to do this" or "I will that you do that." In her eyes that was equivalent to saying "God wills." She did not impose her own will nor did she seek to dominate. But she knew how to accept responsibilities and to make up her mind to act when it was necessary and in the manner which necessity seemed to demand. Whence Catherine's *"Io voglio"* had nothing of domination or tyranny about it, but evidently it jarred the habitual pusillanimity of some people, even of those who see very well what should be done but who, for want of will power, do not do it.

PATIENCE AND FORTITUDE

This humble girl was also patience itself, a patience due to her charity, but which had absolutely nothing in common with the desire to dominate. The Lord had said to her, speaking of the soul that is His true servant: "Loving Me, who am the Supreme Being and worthy to be loved, she loves herself and her neighbor through Me alone, caring only for the glory and praise of My name, which causes her to be patient and strong, to suffer and to persevere." [31] "If the soul elect to love Me, she should elect to endure pains for Me in whatever mode or circumstance I may send them to her. Patience cannot be proved in any other way than by suffering, and patience is united with love, as has been said. Therefore, bear yourselves with manly courage, for unless

[31] *Dialogue,* Chap. LXXVI, p. 143.

you do so, you will not prove yourselves to be spouses of My Truth, and faithful children, nor of the company of those who relish the taste of My honor and the salvation of souls." [32] Patience is the marrow of love, or its humble and gentle countenance.

Nobody was more convinced than Catherine was concerning the truth of this doctrine and nobody gave more proof of patience than she in the difficulties of all kinds that assailed her and sometimes almost submerged her. Hers was a generous soul, preoccupied only in making her will conform in all things with that of God and it was the virtue of patience that carried this resolve into effect. "Oh true and sweet patience," she wrote to Monna Nella, "you are that virtue that is never conquered but always conquers. . . . You dissolve hatred in the heart and all its rancor. You destroy all bitterness against one's neighbor. You lift the heart from all its troubles. For you, heavy burdens and tribulations without number become light. Through you, displeasure changes into sweetness." [33] "Once it becomes patient, the heart is not scandalized nor troubled by anything." [34] "She possesses herself truly in patience. She is a queen who rules impatience and does not allow herself to be overcome by anger." [35]

This is the only domination that Catherine knew and practiced and it did great honor to her charity. She dominated herself in the midst of all her fatigues and tribulations. In fact, her sanctity was only a long patience.

Moreover, it is in the same exalted sense that she praised the supernatural virtue of fortitude, to which patience is united. Here again is revealed the profoundly human spirit in the doctrine of Catherine. "God," she writes to Peter del

[32] *Ibid.,* Chap. V, p. 10.
[34] Letter 304.
[33] Letter 151.
[35] Letter 297.

Monte, "has provided man with a defense so powerful that neither demon nor creature can do him harm—his free will. . . . And He intends that we make use of this weapon that He has given us, so that with it we may resist the blows that we receive from our enemies. . . . If man does not despoil himself of this weapon and if he himself does not place it in the hands of the demon by giving his consent, he will never be conquered." [36]

Doubtless, the use of our freedom in matters that call for the exercise of the supernatural virtue of fortitude requires the grace of God, without which we can do nothing. But grace does not dispense us from the personal effort of collaborating in the work of God. Like discretion and patience, the virtue of fortitude has charity as its principle. Charity is like a summit on which all the virtues have their origin. This is the doctrine of St. Thomas and it is also that of St. Catherine. So we read in one of her letters to Stephen Maconi: "I say it is in the following manner that we are able to acquire the glorious virtue of fortitude and perseverance. If our reason has been strengthened in the blood of Christ, we should renounce ourselves to this sweet and glorious recompense. With the eye of the intellect and the light of holy faith we discover it in the vessel of our soul; we understand that our being comes from God; we see that God restored us to the life of grace in the blood of His only Son and that thus our weakness disappeared. . . . O Blood, . . . you embrace and consume the soul in the furnace of divine charity, that is to say, you consume all that is found in the soul that is not the will of God. . . . O sweetest Blood, you despoil the soul of sensible self-love, which weakens the soul that is clothed in it, and you envelop it with flames of divine charity, . . . for you were shed

[36] Letter 148.

through the ardor of love. That is why love does not exist without fortitude nor fortitude without perseverance, and that is why it strengthens and fortifies in every adversity. . . . Supported by supreme fortitude, you will be strong and persevering and will make the weakness of your own sensibility disappear. In bitterness you will taste sweetness and in the midst of war you will enjoy peace." [37]

Struggles and difficulties are unable to harm the soul that is strengthened by the virtue of fortitude. On the contrary, they provide an opportunity for it to intensify its union with God who is its strength, to prove its love of Him, and to increase its patience, the more so as the gift of fortitude always accompanies the virtue and supplies for its imperfections when necessary. In a letter to Cardinal Bonaventure of Padua, Catherine praises the good effects of the virtue of fortitude: "Can the trials and persecutions of the world make a soul become weak? Assuredly not. On the contrary, the soul draws from them a greater strength, because they are occasions for the soul to rely with much more solicitude on its fortitude. In that way also, the love it has for God is the means of testing and manifesting whether it is a mercenary love or not, whether it tends to self-gratification or not. Creatures cannot weaken it with their ever-recurring persecutions, their injustices, their outrages, their reproaches, their contempt, or their insults. Rather, these things make the soul withdraw more and more from all love of creatures and exercise it in the virtue of patience. Consequently, nothing can cause the soul to weaken, unless man consents to it and separates himself from fortitude. That is true of whatever situation in which a man may find himself, for no situation or circumstance can take God from us. God pays attention to neither the situation nor the place

[37] Letter 195.

nor the time. He is eager only for a holy and sincere desire." [38]

HEROIC LOVE

Such is, in its sweeping lines, St. Catherine's doctrine of love. It is truly the doctrine of a contemplative soul whose contemplation ends in an action that renders it fruitful. For this soul of fire has at the same time a nostalgia for the light. She burns with love of God who is all love, but she does not wish to love Him blindly, in the darkness of sentimentality, and still less in that of sensuality. Unable to contemplate Him face to face here below or to love without measure and without weakening, she wishes at least to know Him as much as is possible for a creature whose intellectual eye has been supernaturally enlarged and fortified by the pupil of faith. It is also in Him that she wishes to know herself, in the light of His creative and redemptive goodness, and not in the deforming mirror of sensible self-love and of human pride. Thus she will be able to partake of His dignity and His infamy and to clothe herself with humility.

But it is not enough to love God in the light; it is necessary that this enlightened and glowing love pass from our heart into our life and there impregnate all our acts, so that the loving contemplation of God illumines our action and makes it fruitful. Thus we see Catherine engrossed in enveloping her life with light and saturating it with love. In order not to walk and act blindly under the impulse of the love of God, of self, and of neighbor, she calls upon prudence, or discretion. She will force herself to do all with judgment, moderation, and balance, as befits an intelligent being made to the image of God who Himself "has regulated all with measure, name, and weight." [39]

[38] Letter 334.   [39] Wisd. 11:21.

Actually, this implies following the path of heroism. On the one hand, the love of God is demanding; on the other hand, love of self and neighbor in God clashes with obstacles of every kind in the daily exercise of virtue where the Christian conscience does not allow a compromise. These obstacles are constant; they spring interiorly from some duty to be accomplished or exteriorly by way of trials from circumstances, associations with men, and even from God Himself. To bear all this demands an unflinching patience and a superhuman fortitude.

Catherine realized that she was encouraged to enter upon this heroic way and to persevere in it, simply because she loved God above all things and depended on His grace that she would not faint on the way. God so loved us that He gave us His only Son. Without Him we can do nothing, but with Him we can do all things. When action seems a burden too heavy to carry, our soul seeks refuge in contemplation, and this laver of light and of love renews our strength to go forward.

It remains for us to see the way in which Catherine's doctrine of love penetrated her private and public life, her intimate relations with God, and her apostolic relations with her neighbor. All the activities of her life marvelously reflect her doctrine. She is filled with light and love because grace perfected her nature extraordinarily. In spite of certain appearances to the contrary, this mystic, who seems lost in God, despises nothing that is truly human and made to the image of God. On the contrary, she strives to divinize it by faith, hope, and charity, and all those supernatural virtues or powers that charity engenders, nourishes, and develops, as well as the gifts which are added to these and enrich them under the inspiration of the Holy Ghost.

In St. Catherine's life as in her writings all is God and

everything seems to spring from her spontaneously. Her acts, inspired by charity, bear the mark of her strong will, just as her writings, inspired by God, bear the mark of her penetrating mind. Her language of action has brilliance of style and variety. A metaphor by which she has conveyed her doctrine applies equally to her own life and it is with this metaphor that we shall finish this chapter.

"Dost thou know how these three virtues stand together? It is as if a circle were drawn on the surface of the earth, and a tree, with an off-shoot joined to its side, grew in the center of the circle. The tree is nourished in the earth contained in the diameter of the circle, for if the tree were out of the earth it would die and give no fruit. Now, consider in the same way, that the soul is a tree existing by love and that it can live by nothing else than love, and that if this soul have not in very truth the divine love of perfect charity, she cannot produce fruit of life, but only of death. It is necessary, then, that the root of this tree, that is, the affection of the soul, should grow in and issue from the circle of true self-knowledge which is contained in Me, who have neither beginning nor end, like the circumference of the circle, for turn as thou wilt within a circle, inasmuch as the circumference has neither end nor beginning, thou always remainest within it.

"This knowledge of thyself and of Me is found in the earth of true humility, which is as wide as the diameter of the circle, that is, as the knowledge of self and of Me (for otherwise the circle would not be without end and beginning, but would have its beginning in knowledge of self and its end in confusion, if this knowledge were not contained in Me). Then the tree of love feeds itself on humility, bringing forth from its side the off-shoot of true discretion, in the way that I have already told thee, from the heart of the tree, that is, the affection of love which is in the soul, and the patience which proves that I am in the soul and the soul in Me. This tree then, so sweetly planted, produces fragrant blossoms of virtue, possessing many scents of great variety, inasmuch as the soul renders fruit of grace and utility to her neighbor, according to the zeal of those who come to receive fruit from My servants. And to Me she renders the sweet odor of glory and praise to My name and thus fulfills the object of her creation.

"In this way, therefore, she reaches the term of her being, that is, Myself, her God, who am eternal life. And these fruits cannot be taken from her without her will, inasmuch as they are all flavored with discretion, because they are all united, as has been said above." [40]

[40] *Dialogue,* Chap. X, p. 20.

CHAPTER 4 ✍

Fullness of Contemplation

FOLLOWING the analysis we have made in the preceding chapter, the reader will observe that Catherine's doctrine is the same in her letters as in the *Dialogue*. It is a doctrine of love revealed to her by God and which she dictated to her disciples during her ecstasies, in the full tide of contemplation. However, there is a striking difference between the *Dialogue* and the letters. In the *Dialogue* it is God who speaks to Catherine and, for the several days that the dictation lasts, teaches her the whole doctrine of love contained in the book. In the letters, on the contrary, it is Catherine who speaks to her correspondents and, as it were, interprets for them the doctrine developed throughout the *Dialogue*. Thus, we have clear proof that the apostolate of Catherine, whose letters are the only direct testimony that has come down to us, sprang from her contemplation. Better still, her contemplation, like her doctrine, was an authentic source of her apostolate.

After having analyzed the doctrine of St. Catherine, it is important to study her contemplation. In this way we shall be in a position to make a more authoritative evaluation of the brilliance and extent of her apostolate. Verily, Catherine is a contemplative soul whose charity overflows into the various forms of the apostolate. In this she shows herself to be truly the daughter par excellence of St. Dominic, that great contemplative who spent the greater part of his nights in prayer in heart-to-heart conversation with God and, after having reduced his body to servitude by penance in order the better to liberate his mind, he knew how to speak only to God or of God.

Let us open the *Dialogue* for a moment and listen to the Lord Himself speaking to Catherine of her father Dominic and of the Order that he founded. It is one of the most moving pages of this inspired book and today more than ever, it is desirable that all the sons and daughters of St. Dominic should there refresh their souls so that they may remain faithful to their contemplative and apostolic vocation—*Contemplata aliis tradere.*

"Now look at the ship of thy father Dominic, My beloved son. He ordered it most perfectly, desiring that his sons should apply themselves only to My honor and the salvation of souls with the light of science, which light he laid as his principal foundation; not, however, being deprived on that account of true and voluntary poverty, but having it also. And as a sign that he had it truly, and that the contrary displeased him, he left as an heirloom to his sons his curse and Mine, if they should hold any possessions either privately or in community, as a sign that he had chosen poverty for his spouse.

"But for his more immediate and personal object he took the light of science, in order to extirpate the errors that had arisen in his time, thus taking upon himself the office of My only-begotten Son, the Word. Rightly he appeared as an apostle in the world and sowed the seed of my Word with much truth and light, dissipating darkness and giving light. He was a light that I gave the world by means of Mary and was placed in the mystical body of the holy Church as an extirpator of heresies. Why do I say by means of Mary? Because Mary gave him his habit. This duty was committed to her by My goodness.

"And at what table does he feed his sons with the light of science? At the table of the Cross, which is the table of holy desire. . . . Dominic does not wish his sons to apply themselves to anything, but to remain at this table and there, with the light of science, seek the glory and praise of My name alone and the salvation of souls. And in order that they might do nothing else, he chose poverty for them, so that they might not have the care of temporal things.

"It is true that some failed in faith, fearing that they would not be provided for, but he, never. Being clothed in faith and trusting with firm confidence in My providence, he wishes his sons to observe obedience and do their duty. And since impure living obscures the eye of the intellect, and not only the eye of the intellect but also that of the body, . . . he imposed on them the third vow of continence, and wishes that all should observe it with true and perfect obedience. . . . So he has rigged his ship with the three ropes of obedience, continence, and true poverty. He made it a royal ship, not obliging his subjects under pain of mortal sin. . . . He provided for those who should be less perfect, for though all . . . are perfect in kind, yet one possesses a higher degree of perfection than another. Yet all, perfect or imperfect, live well in this ship. . . .

"Wherefore, his Order is a delightful garden, broad and joyous and fragrant. . . . Look at my glorious Thomas, who gazed with the gentle eye of his intellect at My Truth, whereby he acquired supernatural light and a science infused by grace, for he obtained it rather by means of prayer than by human study. He was a brilliant light, illuminating his Order and the mystical body of the holy Church and dissipating the clouds of heresy. Look at Peter, virgin and martyr, who by his blood gave light amidst the darkness of many heresies. The heretics hated him so that at last they took his life; yet while he lived he applied himself to nothing but prayer, preaching, disputing with heretics, hearing confessions, announcing the truth, and spreading the faith without any fear. . . . He not only confessed it in his life, but even at the moment of his death, for when he was in his last extremity, having neither voice nor ink, and having received his death-blow, he dipped his finger in his own blood, and this glorious martyr, not having paper on which to write, leaned over . . . and wrote the *Credo* on the ground. His heart burned in the furnace of charity, so that he never slackened his pace nor turned his head back, though he knew that he was to die, for I had revealed to him his death. But like a true knight he fearlessly came forth on to the battlefield. And I could tell thee the same of many others who, though they did not actually experience martyrdom, were martyrs in desire like Dominic. Of a truth, Dominic and Francis were two pillars of the holy Church. Francis with the poverty which was especially his own, . . . and Dominic with his learning." [1]

In the preceding chapter, when presenting the doctrine of Catherine of Siena as contained in the *Dialogue,* we had occasion to compare it with that of St. Thomas and to note that they differed very little, except for the manner of exposition. That of St. Thomas is presented in a more didactic fashion, while that of Catherine is characterized by a more intuitive approach. Humanly speaking, St. Thomas' power of intuition goes hand in hand with the power of reasoning; in St. Catherine it is the power of intuition that dominates. But in the supernatural order, and more properly in

[1] *Dialogue,* Chap. CXXXIX, pp. 312–15.

contemplation, where logic gives place to intuition and where, as Pascal would say, the geometric mind yields to the sensitive mind, St. Catherine joins hands with St. Thomas. They are two contemplative souls of the same lineage, docile to the inspirations of the Holy Ghost. Thanks to His gifts and under the ardent fire of their charity, they succeed in taking possession of the God who dwells in them, if not by seeing Him, at least by sensing His presence and enjoying it ineffably.

How did that occur? That is precisely what we shall attempt to describe, at least in regard to the contemplation of St. Catherine, so that we may show how her contemplation was the immediate and everflowing source of her apostolate. St. Thomas will help us, for this great contemplative was likewise a great theologian who applied himself to examine closely the nature of mystical contemplation in order to determine its causes and effects, while profiting from his personal experiences. With a guide as sure and as well-informed as Thomas, we are certain of not wandering on the way and, in the light of what he said, of understanding better what St. Catherine did.

THE DIVINE INDWELLING

It is around the doctrine of the indwelling of the Holy Ghost in the souls of the just that St. Thomas has constructed his doctrine on contemplation. He first recalls that God, the immediate source of being, is by this title necessarily present in all things by his creative and preserving action.[2] The Lord Himself will sum up this doctrine in a word when He says to St. Catherine of Siena, "I am He who is, you are she who is not." And Catherine will understand immediately that every creature, in order to exist, to live,

[2] *Summa theol.*, Ia, q. 8, a. 3.

and to act, is dependent on the action of the Creator as a stream is dependent on the spring which feeds it or the flames on the fire from which they emanate.

However, in the souls of the just this creative presence of God in all things is enriched by a presence which is much more intimate, from the fact that sanctifying grace, which transforms human nature not by destroying it but by perfecting it, makes it participate in the nature and the very life of God. Then the Holy Ghost dwells personally in the soul of the just. Doubtless, this presence of the Holy Ghost does not exclude that of the Father and the Son, but emphasizes its particular characteristic as a presence of love.[3]

The creative presence of God extends to all things and imposes itself on each one of them at all times, wherever there is an atom of being to be conserved. His loving presence, on the contrary, is realized only in the souls that are in the state of grace and who, by virtue of this state, enjoy loving relations with Him. The Holy Ghost dwells in them in an intimate and permanent manner. He becomes and remains their habitual guest as long as sin does not come to break their relations, and the greater or less intimacy they experience depends practically on the more or less profound manner in which the soul answers by its charity to the love of God.

It remains to be seen what a soul in the state of grace has at its disposal to become aware of the loving presence of God and to enjoy it. The answer to this question introduces us from the outset to the very heart of contemplation. For, according to the unanimous teaching of theologians and the best mystical authors, contemplation consists in "seeing God," not seeing Him face to face as He is in Himself in the splendor of His divine being (this vision is not of earth, but

[3] Cf. *Ibid.*, Ia, q. 43, a. 3.

of heaven), but as He dwells in us through the personal relationship established by sanctifying grace.

Whatever their differences of viewpoint or expression on detailed points, the same theologians and mystical authors who agree in maintaining that contemplation here below consists in seeing God, are likewise in accord in declaring that this vision of God is attained through the veils and shadows of faith, under the influence of charity, and by the instrumentality of the gifts of the Holy Ghost. Furthermore, it can be attained only on the condition that the soul, impelled by charity, enlightened by faith, and governed by supernatural prudence, gives itself with unwearying fidelity to the practice of the moral virtues, purifies its senses by mortification, and works toward the purification of its heart and mind.

For the time being we shall abstract from the moral conditions that are required for a soul in the state of grace to give itself to contemplation. The necessity of a pure heart and mind to see God [4] is so evident that true contemplatives have always vied with each other in zeal to obtain this double purification at any cost. Sometimes it was accomplished at the price of the most heroic virtue and the greatest physical and moral sufferings.

FAITH AND CHARITY

If contemplation requires a special illumination by the gifts of the Holy Ghost in order to see God, why does it also require the exercise of all the theological virtues and in particular that of faith and charity? The reason for this is that without these virtues, which are the diffusion of sanctifying grace into our intellect and our will, the Holy Ghost would not dwell in us. St. Thomas tells us that God is in all

[4] Matt. 5:1.

things by His action, insofar as He unites Himself to them
in giving them existence and preserving them in being. But
God is in the saints through the action of the saints themselves, who attain to God and somehow possess Him
through knowledge and love.[5] He does not dwell everywhere but He is said to dwell only in the just soul through
His grace. And even if the just soul is not actually knowing
or loving God, nevertheless He dwells in it, as long as it
possesses, through grace, the virtues of faith and charity, as
is evident in the case of baptized infants.[6] In the very gift
of sanctifying grace the just man receives at the same time
the Holy Ghost, who comes to dwell in him. Thus, the Holy
Ghost is given and sent.

Faith enables us to believe firmly the truths that God has
revealed and which He teaches us through His Church. But
faith does not make us see God; it only makes us know with
certitude, although in an obscure manner, certain secrets
that it has pleased God to reveal to us about His nature, His
intimate life, and His relations of love with us. God alone
penetrates the depths of these mysteries, but the infallibility
of His testimony guarantees their authenticity. However,
theologians who derive their inspiration from St. Thomas
assure us that saintly souls and mystics, dwelling in the
interior of the luminous circle of faith traced by the hand
of God as He revealed these mysterious truths, have been
able to enrich their abstract knowledge by personal experiences of God, provided they love Him above all things and
enter into intimate union with Him.

But why does charity enjoy the privilege of making God
known in a special manner that does not resort to faith,

[5] St. Thomas, *In II Cor.*, VI, 16, lect. 3; cf. also *Summa theol.* Ia,
q.43, a.3, ad 1um and 2um.
[6] *In II Cor.*, III, 16, lect. 3.

while still remaining enlightened by faith? And how is it possible for the intellect of the believer, under the influence of charity, to be conscious of the intimate and personal relations that the soul has with God and the particular effects that are the savory fruits of these relations?

Charity, says St. Thomas, is friendship.[7] But it is the nature of friendship in general to establish a real and personal union between two friends, and the same thing is true when it is a question of charity between a soul and God. The intellect, even when it takes possession of revealed truths to which it adheres by faith, conceives them in an abstract manner and through them sees God objectively, as the theologians say. But when the will is inflamed by charity it tends to unite itself to God Himself, the divine reality, without any intermediary.

Charity can thus be compared with human love, and personal union with God, the Being who is loved, is its *raison d'être*. The soul loves God only to unite itself to Him, to be one with Him. In the order of human affections, obstacles of all kinds can prevent two friends from being united. When it is a question of the soul that loves God, there can be no obstacle to this union on the part of God, for He is everywhere and is always present by reason of His creative action. "In Him we live and move and are."[8] Or, as St. Thomas says, God is nearer to us than we are to ourselves.[9] Consequently, a man who possesses charity and loves God with all his heart and mind and strength needs only to enter into himself to find God, to unite himself with God and be one with Him, to attain Him really and to embrace Him personally. On the other hand, faith teaches us that God on His part seeks only to facilitate this union, even

[7] *Summa theol.*, IIa IIae, q. 23, a. 1.   [8] Acts 17:28.
[9] *Summa theol.*, Ia., q. 8.

to incite it and render it fruitful. "If anyone love Me, he will keep My word, and My Father will love him and We will come to Him, and will make Our abode with him." [10]

Thus is explained the indwelling of the Holy Ghost in the souls of the just. God, by His creative action, is present in us as in all other things, in order to bring us into existence and to preserve us. He created us out of pure love, through a kind of necessity which great hearts feel of giving themselves entirely. His creative action envelops all His other gifts: those of the Incarnation, of the Redemption, and of predestination. Therefore, on God's part there is no obstacle to our union with Him. If we love Him with the divine friendship which charity causes and if we sincerely try to find Him, all obstacles of every kind are removed. Now we can understand why saintly souls in their contemplation strive with all the force of a will divinized by charity to unite themselves to God and, upon achieving this, praise the sweetness and fruitfulness of this mystic union.

But, and this is an experience common to all contemplatives, the saints do not sing only of their personal union with God. They describe in detail the nature of this union and they reveal to us its secret. In reading their works we note that contemplation led them to see God in a certain manner, to be certain of His presence in them, to hear Him, to taste Him, and to experience His action in them.

The person that we love is truly present in us. He comes to us first by the agreeable impression that we feel under his influence. We find ourselves interiorly adapted to his charms. We take complacence in him, and this sentiment constitutes love. Then desire and pursuit follow and they carry us toward him whom we love so that we may enjoy him effectively and rest in him. Doubtless, the person loved

[10] John 14:23.

always remains outside of us in his substantial reality. Our heart does not identify itself with him such as he is. However, we submit to his action. He is then in us all the same. On the other hand, we are also in the beloved. The proof of this is that we consider as our personal good or evil whatever is good or bad for the one we love. We feel his joys and sorrows as our own. His wishes become ours and his will becomes our own. We become one with him and and look upon our friend as identified with ourselves.[11]

But what is true of all love, of all friendship, is much more true of charity. For here the friend, the being loved, is God Himself, who is all love. God is love, who dwells in us, and, according to St. Paul, "asketh for us with unspeakable groanings." [12] God, as we know created us out of love and through love He became incarnate, suffered, and died on the cross to redeem us. Charity places us in direct and personal contact with this God of love. Under these conditions, how can the effects common to all human friendship fail to be produced between God and a soul who mutually love each other to the point of embracing each other, of being intimately united, and of becoming identified, so to speak? This is a real, personal union, and not merely an ideal, abstract union like that of simple knowledge. Therefore, it cannot but be fruitful. It brings to the soul that experiences it new insights about God and the mysteries that conceal Him like the thick clouds conceal an inaccessible summit.

How can the soul thus united to God in contemplation be aware of these insights and intimate experiences which attain such certitude that faith itself is strengthened and enriched? St. Thomas answers that this cognizance of the intimate relations of the soul with God and of the modal-

[11] Cf. *Summa theol.,* Ia IIae, qq. 8, 9, 45, 180.   [12] Rom. 8:26.

ities which follow them is effected by the inspiration of
the Holy Ghost and by means of the gifts of understanding,
knowledge, and wisdom. These gifts are infused into the
soul at baptism, together with sanctifying grace and the
supernatural virtues. They are permanent, habitual in-
clinations which render the soul docile to the inspirations
of the Holy Ghost.[13]

MYSTICAL CONTEMPLATION

Considered academically and especially as it is presented
in the beautiful and copious volumes that have been devoted to its exposition, contemplation appears to be a very
complicated matter. Actually, it is no more complicated
than life, at least such as biological and medical treatises
present it. Like life, it is basically simple. Thanks be to
God, we can live without even suspecting what the defini-
tion of life is and without having read any of the explanations of biologists. In addition to the ordinary means of
information and defense such as the intellect, memory,
imagination, and senses, man is provided with a host of
instincts, habits, reflexes, and experiences which immediately and infallibly inform him what should be done or
avoided in order not to be exposed to accident, illness, or
death. In the daily life of most men the instinct for preserva-
tion supplies for biological or medicinal knowledge about
life and even surpasses them in certitude.

A child incapable of grasping the intellectual form and
universal application of a first principle as simple as "the
whole is greater than the part," possesses a practical intuition of it. If he is hungry, he does not hesitate in choosing
between a whole apple and only a half. An artistic genius
who has never attended an art institute would have received

[13] Cf. *Summa theol.*, IIa IIae, qq. 8, 9, 45, 180.

from nature an innate sense of the beautiful. He would bear in his heart an overwhelming respect and love for his art and would be in a better position to create a masterpiece than the cleverest technician, who knew all of the secrets of his art but was without inspiration. For genius, even though it must be developed patiently and presupposes sufficient knowledge, is before all else intuitive. The great philosophers, the great scientists, and the great artists are the *voyants* par excellence. They have, as it were, a special sense of reality and are able to enter into direct contact with it without having recourse to the intermediaries of reasoning or technique.

What has been said of an artist is also true of the saints and the virtuous Christian. A just or a chaste man who has spent his life practicing these virtues knows more about them than the most educated of moral theologians, who may have composed several substantial treatises on them. The practice of virtue sharpens the instinct and in all circumstances develops one's intuition of the virtue. In a given case, when there is question of finding an immediate solution for an unforeseen difficulty, the saint's intuition will surpass in rapidity and certitude the demonstrations of the most penetrating theologian.

What is true of the practice of virtue is true also of love. That is why parents are natural educators of their children. A mother who is truly a mother, who has brought the child into the world, nourished and trained him, followed his growth day by day, observed his varied reactions in the daily struggle of life, assisted in the unfolding of his affection, and rejoiced in the gradual development of his intelligence, knows her child better than the highly educated and clever instructors who would attempt to form and educate him by applying the most approved pedagogical methods. The mother will train him better and more surely than the teacher, thanks to her maternal intuitions and the affective knowledge that she has acquired through an experience that is animated by love.

These remarks concerning a certain superiority of intuition over reasoning and of the sensitive spirit over the mathematical spirit are in no way meant to diminish the value of science, demonstration, or technique. We are merely attempting to show what takes place in contemplation, in the intimate relations of a soul with God. The "multiplication of elements," of which the detractors of Scholasticism complain, that is, adding to sanctifying grace the supernatural virtues and to the virtues, the gifts of the Holy Ghost, correspond to realities of which one is obliged to take account. This is especially true when all mystics agree on these realities and theologians are in accord regarding their psychological explanation.

St. Thomas insists that the soul must be endowed with habits that permit it to receive and follow with ease the inspirations of the Holy Ghost.[14] "Supernatural knowledge in us is based on faith. . . . Therefore, some things must be proposed for belief by man, not as seen, but as heard, and to these things he assents by faith. But faith is first and principally about the first truth, secondarily about certain considerations about creatures, and ultimately it extends to the direction of human acts as it works through charity. . . . Regarding the things proposed for belief by faith, two things are required of us: first, that they be penetrated or grasped by the intellect, and this belongs to the gift of understanding; secondly, that man should judge these things correctly and that he should realize that he ought to adhere to these things and avoid their opposites. If this judgment

[14] *Ibid.*, Ia IIae, q.68, a.3.

is concerned with divine things, it belongs to the gift of wisdom; if it is concerned with created things, it belongs to the gift of knowledge; and if it applies to individual actions, it belongs to the gift of counsel." [15]

Therefore, the three gifts of understanding, knowledge, and wisdom are the principles of contemplation. Even in this life the eye which is purified by the gift of understanding can see God in some manner.[16] Contemplation is a simple gaze, an intuition of the spirit regarding divine truth.[17] It is the function of wisdom to contemplate divine things, as it is the function of the gift of knowledge to lead us from effects to the contemplation of God.[18] These three gifts have charity for their foundation and their common bond.[19] Contemplation is a knowledge which has its beginning and its end in love. The gifts that it requires are essentially an increase of intellectual light, but a light that springs from charity. "The philosophers and the saints," remarks St. Thomas ingeniously, "do not understand the contemplative life in the same way. For the philosophers, the aim of contemplation is wisdom (*sapere*) or metaphysical knowledge, . . . and this is for them supreme happiness. . . . But the contemplation of which the theologians treat consists rather in savoring (*sapore*) than in wisdom, rather in love and sweetness than in the act of contemplation itself. If, then, anyone study in order to know, but not to be edified or to grow in divine love, let him know that he is leading the contemplative life of the philosophers and not that of which theologians treat." [20]

In summary, with the saints, love leads to contemplation and contemplation ends in love. One can contemplate God

[15] *Ibid.*, IIa IIae, q.8, a.6.   [16] *Ibid.*, Ia IIae, q.69, a.2, ad 3um.
[17] *Ibid.*, IIa IIae, q.180, *passim.*   [18] *Ibid.*, IIa IIae, q.180, a.4.
[19] *Ibid.*, Ia IIae, q.68, a.5.   [20] *In Canticum*, I.

only on the condition that he love God, but the saints contemplate Him in order to love Him more. When a contemplative soul, with its loving will saturated by charity, embraces God Himself in its inmost part where He dwells by love, and when God, in virtue of this divine familiarity which is established between them, makes the soul feel His presence, inundates it with joy and consolations or, on the contrary, tests the soul in an ineffable and unforeseen manner, the gifts of the Holy Ghost which that soul possesses in a habitual state first render the soul docile to the divine inspirations and then make it vibrate to the breath of divine love which passes over it. Then the gifts of understanding, knowledge, and especially wisdom, which are the antennae of charity, vibrate under the impulse of the Holy Ghost. Intuitively, each in its own way experiences all the divine reality which this union with God through charity connotes.

At this moment the soul is so certain of not being deceived in regard to God's action in it that this certitude, thanks to the gift of understanding which causes it, reacts on its faith, not to make it see revealed truths more clearly, but to make it feel divinely, without being able to demonstrate it, that there is nothing more certain than those truths. Nothing is as certain, profound, and true as the divine mysteries in which the soul believes. The most beautiful spiritual treatises in the world would be incapable of communicating to the soul a similar awareness of the presence of God.

Once immersed in God, fused in Him, and certain of its union with Him, the soul feels or sees, thanks to the gift of knowledge, that outside of God no created thing is of importance in itself. Everything in this world that love has created exists only by God and for God. Sin saddens but does not scandalize such a soul. Its sense of the love of God reveals to it that evil in general and sin in particular have their place in the world, their reason for being. In the symphony of the universe, all these dissonances resolve finally in the love of God and for His glory.

The gift of wisdom makes the soul taste the love of God directly and in a penetrating manner. Through it, the soul sees in a simple gaze all the divine mysteries that are attached to it. It has a direct intuition of the sovereign goodness of God who, because of the fullness of His love and a kind of need to give Himself and to let certain creatures participate in His being, His life, and His glory, created man in the state of grace and innocence. Then, when sin was committed, He became incarnate and suffered and died on the cross in order to save sinners. He willed to live in the souls of the just and while safeguarding their liberty, He draws them to Himself to immerse them in love and inundate them with peace. The holy soul, united to God by charity in contemplation, sees and feels all these things intensely, invincibly, without reasoning, and in a simple gaze charged with love.

But before reaching this state, the soul must purify itself and the Holy Ghost must purify its senses, will, and intellect. This higher purification should remove from the heart every affection that is incompatible with charity and should relieve the mind of all images that encumber it, even those restricted concepts that prevent the soul from knowing God as He is in Himself. The Holy Ghost thus raises the contemplative soul above the level of abstractions, for contemplation is a simple gaze, an intuition which passes beyond the world of images and ideas. The soul, freed from all dross and under the influence of charity, unites itself to God and is illumined by divine wisdom. It embraces God in His profundity and in His transcendence. Many words, images, and ideas would be necessary to attempt to explain to those who have not seen Him what the soul has seen of God in her contemplation. The writings of the best informed mystics and their richest experiences are proof of this. But in order to see God in this manner, the saintly soul has need only to love Him with a pure, ardent, and disinterested love and to open itself wide to the inspirations of His Spirit.

CATHERINE AS A CONTEMPLATIVE

One day St. Catherine of Siena spoke to her spiritual director, Raymond of Capua, about a soul who loved her Creator. When she told him that this soul no longer saw herself, that she no longer loved for herself or others, and that she no longer remembered herself or any other creature, Raymond asked for an explanation of these words. Catherine answered: "The soul who already sees her nothingness and who knows that all her being is in the Creator, completely abandons herself and all creatures and immerses herself entirely in the Creator. He becomes the principal end of all her operations. She feels that she has found in Him every good and every perfect happiness and she no longer wishes to withdraw from Him in any way whatever. This vision of love, which grows clearer each day, so transforms the soul in God that her thoughts, her intellect, her heart, and her memory no longer have any other object than God or the things of God. She remembers herself and others only in God.

"Whoever plunges into the sea and swims under water sees and touches only the waters of the sea and what they enclose. Outside of these waters he sees nothing, touches nothing, feels nothing. If exterior objects are reflected in the water, only then can he see them, but only in the water and in the degree in which they are reflected there and not otherwise. Such is the just and well-ordered love one ought to have for self and for all creatures. In this love there is never error, for the divine law is necessarily its measure. It does nothing to make us wish to be estranged from God and, consequently, it is always in God that it functions and develops."

It would be difficult to find in Catherine's writings a passage that gives a more exact idea of her contemplation, of the vision of love which she had attained and which made her feel God as her supreme good and perfect happiness. Becoming clearer each day, it so transformed her soul into God that it no longer had any other object than God. She saw everything in Him and she saw Him in everything. If one can rightly speak of a transforming union when describing one of the peaks of contemplation, it would surely apply to Catherine, who used the expression herself to designate the principal effect of her vision of love in union with God. By what paths did she have to pass in order to ascend this height where she saw God in a simple gaze, by an intuition of her soul under the influence of charity, and by surrendering herself with all her powers to the inspirations of the Holy Ghost?

We must not expect to see the contemplative life of St. Catherine develop methodically, step by step, as one sees it unfold chapter by chapter in a complete treatise on the mystical life. Even when in the *Dialogue* she expresses the doctrine of life that God inspired in her, she is only mildly interested in giving it the style of a didactic treatise. Intellectually speaking, Catherine has none of the teacher in her; she expounds but she does not prove. She tells what she sees and the way in which she sees it, and she does not fear to repeat. She fears to touch upon those difficult matters that concern God, His nature, His inner life, His relations of love with us, and our relations of love with Him by faith, hope, and charity, the supernatural virtues, and the gifts of the Holy Spirit. Even more, she is fearful of not repeating enough. In this regard she exhibits a delicate spirit of finesse and incomparable pedagogical qualities.

It is useless to search in Catherine's life for a line of conduct in which we would see her advance progressively from the active to the passive purification of the senses and ultimately to that of the heart and intellect, advancing spiritually from childhood to adolescence and from adolescence to maturity through the purgative, illuminative, and the unitive phases. All these aspects of the contemplative life are based on reason and we see them verified, in varying degrees and in a more or less orderly fashion, not only in the writings of the most authoritative mystics, but more fundamentally in their lives. However, the contemplative life is more dependent upon the work of God than upon that of the soul. The actuation of the special graces which contemplation requires is entirely under God's control. It is He who decides the starry flight of a soul that aspires to contemplate Him. It is He who determines whether the soul will advance slowly or in great strides, with the plodding steps of the ox or with the magnificent sweep of the eagle that soars above the mountain peaks.

What is striking in the life of St. Catherine is the habitual way in which God intervened directly in her life from her earliest childhood to draw her to Himself. At the age of six she has a vision of the Savior, who blesses her. "From this date," says Raymond of Capua, "our little child manifested by her virtues and manners a remarkable wisdom and the maturity of a person advanced in years. Her acts no longer seemed to be those of a child, nor even of a young girl, but those of a mature woman. The fire of divine love had been ignited in her heart and the flame of this virtue illumined her intellect, inflamed her will, strengthened her memory, and, being translated to her external acts, placed everything under the rule of the divine law. . . . She sought out solitary places and secretly scourged her little body with a small cord. Completely abandoning pleasures, she devoted herself assiduously to prayer and meditation. . . . She became more silent from day to day and diminished her daily nourishment."

The future contemplative is already seen in the child of six. First there is the vision of our Lord, whom she will vow to take for her spouse a year later. Then, under the influence of the divine love that was aroused in her by this vision, a complete change of her life occurs, characterized by a practice of Christian virtues which is not usual among children. She experiences a need for solitude in order to give herself to prayer and meditation. Her life becomes a life of penance in which silence, the discipline, abstinence, and fasting play an important role.

Nine or ten years later, when Catherine was about fifteen years of age, the greatly desired habit of St. Dominic was received in the chapel of the *Mantellate* in the church of the Friars Preachers. This was the occasion of a new advance along the way of contemplation and in the practice of the moral virtues which lead to it.

As a result of her meditations on the love of God, a new idea entered her mind and won her heart. She understood and felt at the same time that the love of neighbor is inseparable from the love of God and that God Himself has given us striking proof of this in the Person of the incarnate Word, our Lord Jesus Christ. By making man an intelligent and free creature, God had given him at creation all that was necessary to make him an image of the Creator and by creat-

ing man in the state of grace and innocence, He endowed
man with all the means of approaching God in this world
and of possessing Him eternally in the next. Far from arrest-
ing the flow of God's creative love, original sin had, on the
contrary, increased it tenfold, in the sense that God gave to
the world His only-begotten Son to satisfy for sin and to save
sinners. The Word became incarnate and, after thirty-three
years spent on earth in the practice of the most eminent human and divine virtues and in the most intimate union with
His Father whom He continued to contemplate face to face,
He died of love on the cross, shedding His precious blood to
the last drop for the salvation of souls.

In view of all this, how can we love God, how can we unite
our wills with His unless, like Him, we love our neighbor?
Catherine's Dominican vocation was born of such reflections. If, under the inspiration of the Holy Ghost, she had
insisted so strongly that she be permitted to enter the
Dominican Order, it was for the love of souls. She became a
Dominican in order to collaborate with our Lord, her
Spouse, in the salvation of souls and thus to give God an un-
deniable and living proof of the disinterested love she bore
Him. Christ's love of souls appeared to her as a radiation of
the love of God. She realized that the more she loved God,
the more intimately she possessed Him in contemplation,
the more she would feel herself impelled by the overwhelming urge to make Him known and loved around her and to
lavish on her neighbor the overflow of her contemplation.

Like her father, St. Dominic, whose livery she wore, she
would gradually train herself to speak only of God or to
God. Our Lord would then be for her what He was for St.
Dominic—her model in all things. He would enter into
her life as a matter of course and would never leave it. He
would manifest Himself to her so frequently in a sensible

manner that He would seem to be her true spiritual director. He would personally guide her along the road to perfection which she had pledged herself to follow.

"In taking the habit of the Sisters of Penance," remarks Raymond of Capua, "Catherine did not pronounce the three principal vows of the religious life. Her state did not permit it. . . . Nevertheless, she had in her heart the firm resolution of observing them perfectly. Six years previously she had already made a vow of virginity, taking Jesus Christ as her only spouse. Once a tertiary, she wished to submit herself in everything to the director of the fraternity, to the prior of the Dominican convent, and to her confessor. Before she died, she confessed to her spiritual father that she did not recall failing in obedience a single time."

At this point Raymond of Capua becomes indignant with certain detractors of her sanctity who, "with a tongue as biting as it is untruthful," had maintained the contrary. He places the blame on the shoulders of indiscreet directors who, since they understood nothing of the exceptional gifts that heaven had bestowed on Catherine, "wished absolutely to lead her by ordinary paths, without honoring the special presence of the sovereign Majesty who was directing her along a marvelous way. Nonetheless, they continually saw clear signs of this presence."

Raymond alludes here to the visions and miracles of Catherine which were already becoming more numerous. But he notes with a suggestion of contempt that those indiscreet directors imitated the Pharisees and imputed all these signs to the devil and not to God. According to the authentic testimony of Raymond, it is clear that at that time—after her entry into the Dominican Order—Catherine was already living in the presence of God. Although she had not reached the perfection she would attain later, her vision of love had already begun.

Among the signs of the presence of the sovereign Majesty in Catherine, Raymond mentions her visions. We shall speak more of these, but there are other signs, more common to contemplatives and more evident to observers. They are the visible proof of a charity which is purified, of a penetrating love that one finds at the beginning and end of all contemplation. We would speak, therefore, of the heroic practice of the virtues and of that which in mystical language is called the purification of the senses by penance and which gradually leads to the purification of the heart and of spirit as the soul advances in holiness.

Catherine would sometimes exhort herself by saying: "Now that you have entered religion, you ought not to live as you have lived up to now. The worldly life is past. This is a new life, the religious life, and its rule must necessarily govern you. You must clothe yourself in sovereign purity and surround yourself with it on all sides, as your white tunic signifies. You must be completely dead to the world; your black mantle shows you this plainly. Therefore, mark well what you do. It is the narrow way, where so few walk, that you must follow."

Once re-instated in her room in her father's house, Catherine buried herself in solitude. Her family had driven her from it previously, but they now permitted her the greatest freedom of action. But she spoke to no one except her confessor, and then only in confession. According to the confessor, who recorded it in writing, this continual silence in the solitude of her room lasted three years. She left her room only to go to church. Between times, she kept vigil and prayed in the cell of her heart, under the gaze of the sovereign majesty of God, in whose presence she kept herself constantly through prayer and meditation.

Raymond reports that it was at that time, as he learned from St. Catherine's lips, that her relationship with Jesus Christ, her Spouse, began and increased. In her eyes He was the living incarnation of God's love for men, since He became man only to save them and He died on the cross that they might have eternal life. As soon as she retired into solitude, Jesus came to seek her out and instruct her fully in all those things that would be useful for her soul. "My Father," she said to Raymond, "take it as an absolute and certain truth that none of those things that concern the ways of salvation have ever been taught to me by anyone, either man or woman. He who instructed me is my Lord and Master in person, my incomparable Spouse, the sovereign charm of my soul, the Lord Jesus Christ. Either by His inspirations or by manifest apparitions, He spoke to me as I speak to you now."

Above all, our Lord taught Catherine the subtle art of distinguishing a true vision from a false one and once that was done, He appeared to her frequently. It would be difficult, she said to Raymond of Capua, to find two persons who had as frequent communication with each other as she had with her Spouse. During her prayers, her meditations, her readings, her vigils, and her sleep, at any moment, in one way or another, Jesus would manifest Himself to her in a sensible way and console her.

It can be seen that Catherine was at a good school if she wanted to be initiated into the secrets of contemplation. Our Lord personally taught her the ways to follow to arrive at that state, which she calls the ways of salvation. In the depths of her soul the Holy Ghost first revealed the divine secrets to her under a doctrinal form that was suited to the nature of her intellect and then under a contemplative form better adapted to the aspirations and needs of her heart.

From the moment that Catherine entered the Dominican Order and God called her to the apostolate, it was also necessary for her to possess the light of her father in religion and, like him, to know sacred doctrine in order to diffuse it around her in the souls destined to come under her influence. And since she could not learn from books, God Himself took charge of revealing it to her.

However, doctrine is one thing and contemplation is another. A true son of St. Dominic should succeed in fusing the two by passing sacred doctrine through the fire of charity during his contemplation so that, like the sun, his preaching may both enlighten minds and inflame hearts. Then only will he be an apostle. In fact, the apostolate in a Dominican soul is born of the union of a mind filled with doctrine and a heart filled with charity and kept in habitual contact with God by contemplation. *Contemplata aliis tradere.*

At least this is the way in which Catherine exercised her apostolate and that is why it was so fruitful and so lasting. Animated by an intrepid faith and fortified by sound doctrine, after spending hours in contemplation with God and with a heart still warm from this immediate contact and a mind illumined by what the Holy Ghost had permitted her to see, to feel, and to understand regarding the divine mysteries, she would then dictate those letters which are so remarkable for their warmth and clarity. According to her disciples, who frequently witnessed this state of "volcanic eruption" in which she seemed like another Moses coming out of the burning bush where he had been in the presence of God, it was marvelous to hear her speak out of the abundance of her heart. In fact, as befits an apostle, it was no longer she but God who spoke by her mouth.

We do not have to review the doctrine that God Himself revealed to Catherine. Its outlines were traced in the preceding chapter. However, a question of no little importance arises in regard to this matter and perhaps its solution will help us to see more clearly into Catherine's vocation, which was at once contemplative and apostolic. One may rightly ask why God, who called her to the contemplative life and revealed Himself to her in so secret and original a manner in her contemplation, judged it wise to place at the disposal of an intelligent but illiterate woman (as were most of the women of her time) a theological doctrine such as she expounds throughout the *Dialogue*. But God Himself had answered this question when He told Catherine what He thought of the Order of Preachers to which she belonged. "Your Father Dominic," He said to her, "wished that his sons should apply themselves only to My honor and the salvation of souls by the light of science. This light he wished to make the principal object of his Order. . . . His office was that of the Word, My only begotten Son. . . . He was a light which I gave the world by means of Mary, placed in the mystical body of the holy Church to extirpate heresies." [21]

A son of St. Dominic worthy of the name and faithful to his vocation as a Friar Preacher must possess this light and have a thorough knowledge of sacred science so that he may teach souls. Christ Himself, the Word of God, whose office Dominic filled, spent three years teaching sacred doctrine to His apostles and adapting it to their intelligence before sending the Holy Spirit to them. Then, on Pentecost, in a moment of sublime inspiration and illumination, at one stroke He made them both contemplatives and apostles.

Having established the general inter-relationship of Cath-

[21] *Dialogue,* Chap. CXXXIX.

erine's doctrine and contemplation in view of her apostolate, we must return to her contemplation and try to show in what profound sense this daughter of St. Dominic was a contemplative. To accomplish this, we have her writings and a number of facts characteristic of her life, which have been transmitted by her biographers.

We have seen earlier, with St. Thomas, that the contemplative life is formed around the presence of God in us: the creative and loving presence of the Holy Ghost. But there is no more striking fact in the life of Catherine, and none on which her biographers have insisted so much, than that of her intimate and habitual union with God. The three years of rigorous solitude in her room, which followed her reception of the Dominican habit, during which time she spoke to no one except her confessor, were spent in the presence of God. She was occupied only in knowing Him and knowing herself in Him, in contemplating her own nothingness in the resplendent mirror of the divine being, in rising above the area of speculative abstractions in which the intellect grasps something of God in revealed truths, to unite herself to God in charity and to see Him, under the influence of the Holy Ghost, in a simple gaze or divine intuition of the intellect.

The beautiful and rich doctrine of Catherine, revealed to her by God, confirmed her faith in the sovereign goodness of God. Without doubting for an instant, she believed that God is love and that through love He created us; that He became incarnate in the Person of the Word and redeemed us on the cross by shedding His blood to the last drop. Having opened heaven to us, where we can eternally enjoy the beatific vision, it is likewise through love that He dwells personally in us. Catherine believed all these things without faltering. But her charity was not satisfied with believing; she wanted to see. Her love was not content with abstractions; she hungered for reality. Her faith seemed to reach beyond the framework of revealed truths. She wished to possess God as completely as possible in this world; she wished to contact Him directly and embrace Him personally with all the strength of a will that was aflame with divine love and impregnated with charity.

"Where do we know God and where do we know ourselves?" she writes to Nicholas, a hermit at Florence. "In the interior of our soul," she answers. "For we must enter into the cell of self-knowledge and open the eye of our intellect, of that intellect of which faith is the pupil, by ridding it of all designs of self love. . . . The goodness of God we know in ourselves, by seeing ourselves created to His image and likeness so that we might share in His infinite and eternal happiness, and then, having been deprived of grace by the sin of the first man, re-created in grace in the blood of His only-begotten Son. O inestimable love! To ransom the slave, You have given us the Son; to give us life, You have taken death on Yourself. Thus we see that He is the sovereign and eternal goodness and that He loves us ineffably, for if He did not love us, He would not have given us such a Redeemer." [22]

But it is not enough to know that God is infinitely good, even though this knowledge is possessed by an intellect enlightened by faith. We must experience this goodness in ourselves, we must feel it by answering love with love and, as Catherine says, by casting ourselves into the fiery love of God and even into God Himself, whose love makes Him dwell in us. "Certainly," she writes to Bartholomew and James, hermits at Campo Santo in Pisa, "I am not astonished that the saints were in no way blinded by self-love, but

[22] Letter 78.

were entirely immersed in the knowledge of the goodness of God and in the fire of His ardent charity. . . . Consider the boundless fire of Lawrence who, from the grill answered the taunts of the despot. . . . 'Is there not enough fire for you, Lawrence?' 'No,' he answered, 'for the interior fire of an ardent love is such that it extinguishes the fire outside.' . . . The soul is purified in this sweet fire and you will find the goodness of God perfect in you. By the knowledge of this sovereign goodness, when the soul is drowned in an abyss of love that is so profound that it sees God in itself, the eye of the intellect opens and sees, the memory retains, and the will tends to love whatever He Loves." [23]

In reading through Catherine's letters, one could multiply indefinitely passages of this type. All of them flow from this basic statement: "We must know God in order to love Him, but we must especially love God to know Him better." It is indispensable to know God through faith in order to love Him. And the eye of the intellect will never be opened sufficiently to meditate on the divine mysteries of faith. But to love God, to attain to God Himself who has revealed these truths to us and to attain not only what these truths teach us of Him, but to attain Him as He is in us through the indwelling, where our charity embraces Him and unites Him to us immediately, that is, for the saints, the last word of the knowledge of God here on earth.

If one considers the truths proposed for our belief, the knowledge of God through faith is the same for all, since all, relying on the infallible word of God, are bound to believe what God has revealed and what the Church teaches to all without distinction. But to this knowledge of God through faith, which is a grace of God in each one of us and whose object is, so to speak, imposed on all the faithful from

[23] Letter 134.

without, there is a way of adding another knowledge which is interior and mysterious but more vivid and more intimate. This knowledge of God is born of the personal relations effected by the soul's love of God, of the direct and immediate contact of a loving will with the love of God personified in the Person of the Holy Ghost who dwells within us. Catherine's life was an unceasing pursuit for this twofold knowledge of God through faith and love.

No one has ever insisted more than Catherine did in the *Dialogue* on the need for a charity enlightened by faith and a faith enlivened by the fire of love. Although every Christian is bound to strive for an enlightened faith, this obligation is especially binding on the apostle, whose vocation consists precisely in clarifying the faith of Christians. A true daughter of St. Dominic would feel obliged to insist on this point, and Catherine did not fail to do so. But it is not enough for a Christian or an apostole to be a light. Under pain of possessing a dead faith or of becoming an extinguished candle, as Catherine says,[24] the soul must possess a faith that is vivified by charity, which alone makes good works and the practice of all the virtues meritorious.[25]

Catherine applied herself energetically to enlighten her faith in order to advance in the knowledge of God. She loved to discuss the truths of faith with competent theologians such as Bartholomew Dominici. But she preferred to receive directly from God those shafts of light which she would receive at any moment. One has only to read the *Dialogue* to see how God answered her yearnings. Any solid doctrine that could project light on Catherine's faith to help her know God through revealed truths was given her by God. But He did still more. He lavished on her in contemplation all the intuition of divine mysteries that the loving

[24] Cf. *Dialogue,* Chap. CX.   [25] *Ibid.,* Chap. III.

awareness of God could add to the light and certainty of her faith. It is astonishing to note the rapid progress Catherine made in the knowledge of God and self and the profound changes which resulted in her life.

This saintly and apostolic soul, who loved God with her whole heart and whom God loved so dearly, who lived constantly in His presence and enjoyed His love and graces, far from being inflated by pride, drew a lesson in humility from her extraordinary favors. She saw clearly that God is He who is but she is one who is not; that were it not for His creative love she would not even exist; that without His redeeming love she would be nothing but sin; that if she loved God it was only because of God that she was able to do so and only through the blood of His Son that she had been purified; that if she practiced virtue for the love of God—all the virtues of her state in life—it was due to the efficacy of His grace, since He enabled her to will and to will freely whatever God wills.

Her charity, however it manifested itself—toward God, self, or neighbor,—was nourished by her humility.[26] The more she realized her nothingness in God [27] and the more she felt her absolute dependence on Him, the more deeply she felt the need to plunge herself into His sovereign goodness. She lost herself there in order to find herself more fully, by adding to her faith an experimental knowledge of the divine goodness which the Holy Ghost enabled her to experience in her contemplation through His gifts.

This love of God, which she nourished with humility and from which she drew such an excess of grace, was also a fruitful source of moral action. Convinced that she was nothing apart from God and could accomplish nothing without His grace, she very prudently set herself to conform her will

[26] *Ibid.*, Chap. IV.   [27] *Ibid.*, Chap. IX.

with His in all things. Loving God with such intensity, she hated in herself whatever could paralyze the practice of virtue or set up an obstacle between her soul and God— pride, self-love, or sensuality.

According to the teaching of the *Dialogue,* a teaching vivified by love as her faith was vivified in contemplation, she accepts with gladness all the pains God sends her. Aflame with zeal for the glory of God and experiencing an intense hunger for souls, Catherine runs to the table of the holy Cross. She desires to suffer pain, to endure a thousand fatigues in the service of her neighbor, to acquire virtue, and to bear in her body the wounds of Christ. The love of the Crucified that burns within her is manifested in her contempt of self, in the joy she feels in suffering, and in her welcome of the trials and pains God sends her, no matter whence they come or how He sends them. For her, as for the beloved sons of God, pain is joy. Their real pain comes from the joys, the consolations, and the pleasures that the world sometimes wishes to give them.[28]

To these pains of all kinds which God heaps upon her, she adds others of her own in order to be complete mistress of her own body. Raymond tells us that she reached a point where she fasted and abstained from all nourishment and that she became ill when, in obedience to her directors, she consented to take some nourishment. Daily Communion was sufficient food for her. She prolonged her vigils until she slept only a quarter of an hour daily, spending the rest of the time in intimate union with God. "The more a soul loves God," she once told Raymond, "the more she feels a holy hatred of her sensuality. . . . She exerts all her efforts, not to kill the life of the senses, but to preserve it from the flames of corruption. But that is not accomplished

[28] Cf. *Ibid.,* Chap. LXXVIII.

without a long and bitter war against sensuality." Thus Catherine succeeded in living continually in the presence of God, in an intimate union with Him where spiritual joys and consolations alternated with bitter trials. These bitter-sweet experiences are common in the lives of the mystics.

Raymond of Capua, who was a witness of the numerous ecstasies that were caused by the vision of love during her contemplation, heard her say that she had seen the secrets of God: *Vidi arcana Dei.* When he asked her to explain what she meant, she answered: "It is impossible. I am so conscious of the inadequacy of words to explain this sight that I believe I would be blaspheming in some way by my words. There is such an abyss between the concepts of an intellect that is ravished, illumined, and strengthened by God and that which words are able to express that they would seem to be a contradiction. Therefore, nothing can persuade me to tell you at this time what I have seen. It is ineffable."

Such was Catherine's contemplation. It was an unbroken gaze of love in which the gift of wisdom particularly enabled her, through the power of the Holy Ghost, to taste and see God directly, so far as a soul can see Him here on earth, and also to experience His loving presence in her. St. Thomas says that the contemplation that is produced by the gifts of understanding and wisdom sometimes results in detaching the soul from the operation of the senses.[29] This is the corporeal ecstasy. The time came in Catherine's life when her days and nights were filled with ecstasies and visions. She gave the impression of living habitually in a world above the earth, yet without ever losing sight of the earth, of the conditions in which human beings lived, or of the apostolic vocation to which God would one day invite her when He would ask her, as a true daughter of St. Dominic, to leave

[29] Cf. *De Veritate,* q. 10, a. 11, *sed contra.*

her cell in order to bring truth to souls and to fill their hearts with the overflow of her contemplation.

MYSTICAL PHENOMENA

As to Catherine's visions, the following is the testimony of Raymond of Capua: "I found four volumes written by Brother Thomas, Catherine's confessor, and filled with magnificent visions and unheard-of revelations." Unfortunately, these volumes or note-books of Thomas della Fonte, in which he kept a daily record of the marvels of which he was an eye-witness, are no longer extant. But we have strong reason to think they are recorded substantially but anonymously in the *Supplement* of Caffarini, for in this work we find expressed in the same words the facts that Raymond tells us he copied from the writings of Thomas della Fonte. It will be recalled that Thomas was Catherine's confessor from the day she received the habit in 1363 until the appointment of Raymond in 1374.

Raymond has countless reasons to speak of "magnificent visions" and of "unheard-of revelations." In fact, there are so many visions of such an extraordinary kind that if one did not know the prudence and sincerity of Thomas della Fonte, which other witnesses such as Bartholomew Dominici vouch for, one would be tempted to question them. In addition to this, we have the testimony of Catherine herself, which Raymond invokes repeatedly during the description of her visions. And how can one doubt the sincerity of Catherine, whom Jesus had taught how to distinguish between false visions and true visions? How can one refuse to admit these visions when he learns of the familiar intercourse that had been established daily between Catherine and God during her contemplation?

However, we do not intend to pause here, for the greater

part of Catherine's visions, for example, those of the Blessed Virgin, St. John the Evangelist, St. Paul, St. Mary Magdalen, and St. Dominic, have no direct bearing on her contemplation. Nevertheless, we must mention the frequent visits she received from our Lord, her Spouse, who made Himself her ordinary guide in the contemplative life. Catherine herself admitted to Raymond that no words could express the intimate communion between herself and our Lord, dating especially from the moment when she detached herself completely from the world to take refuge in silence and contemplation.

She concentrated all the love she had for God on the person of our Lord. As the teaching in the *Dialogue* bears witness, when the Eternal Father revealed to Catherine the absolute gratuity of the act of creation, she was overwhelmed, but she realized more and more that once He had entered on the path of love for us, God would not rest content. Other acts would follow to astound the world with the extent of their generosity. The Incarnation and, above all, the Redemption seemed to her the inaccessible peaks of sovereign goodness. When she thought of the enormous price—the price of His blood—that the salvation of souls and their redemption from sin had cost the incarnate Word, her heart beat as if it would break. In the incarnate Word she saw divine love incarnate under the form of the God-made-Man, our Lord Jesus Christ. She contemplated God through the sacred person of Christ. More than ever, she chose Jesus for the Spouse of her soul and Jesus Himself consented to take her as His spouse. He was her support in temptation, her model in suffering, and her guide on the road to perfection.

Raymond tells us that one day Satan mobilized his odious battalions against Catherine. They surrounded her on all sides in order to deprive her of all help and weaken the sources of her strength. They began with temptations of the flesh, and not only did they send dreams to trouble the mind of the Saint with impure images and phantasms while she slept, but they had recourse to external visions as well. To do this, they assumed airy bodies and filled Catherine's vision with all manner of lewd gestures and actions performed in every conceivable fashion. The pen shudders to recount such combats, but the victorious outcome will have an incomparable charm for pure souls.

Catherine answered the obscene and crafty taunts of the devils with an increase of corporal penances and lengthened vigils, saying simply: "I put my trust in our Lord Jesus Christ and not in myself." The tempter could obtain from her no other answer, and Catherine continued her penances or buried herself in prayer.

However, a still more terrible trial was added to this one. Jesus, her Spouse, who used to visit her so often, suspended His visits and seemed to withdraw from her. But Catherine held fast, fought as well as she could, and, docile to the teaching of the Savior, answered the tempter who harassed her: "I have chosen sufferings for my consolation and I will bear them with joy in the name of the Savior, for as long a time as it pleases His Majesty."

At these words, Raymond tells us, the troop of demons were confounded and routed. A brilliant light, falling from above, illumined the whole room and Christ crucified appeared to her, covered with His blood. Then, assuming another form, He approached Catherine and comforted her. "Where were you, Lord," she asked Him, "when my heart was tormented with so many ignominies?" "I was in your heart," Jesus answered, "protecting your heart against your enemies. . . . So, My daughter, because you have faithfully combatted, not by your own strength but by Mine, you have merited an increase of grace. Henceforth I shall appear to you more frequently and more intimately."

As Jesus was Catherine's support in her temptations, He was also her model in suffering. Catherine compared the blood of Jesus to a salutary bath into which she plunged her soul to revive her strength. We are astounded at the spectacle of all the suffering that Catherine accepted or sought with such ardent love. We shall mention only one incident which symbolizes all the others. Although it happened late in Catherine's life, when she was already engaged in the active apostolate, nevertheless it casts a clear light on her whole life and especially on the intimacy of the relations that had been established between our Lord and His faithful spouse after her great temptation. Catherine herself narrated the incident to Raymond.

The Savior of the world appeared to her, holding in His right hand a diadem of gold ornamented with pearls and precious jewels, and in his left hand, a crown of thorns. "Choose," He said, "whether you will have the diadem in this world and the crown of thorns in the world to come, or the crown of thorns here, and the diadem hereafter." Catherine answered: "I wish above all else to unite myself in this life to Your blessed Passion and to have my consolation in suffering for You." She took the crown of thorns in her hands and pressed it down on her head so tightly that the thorns pierced her head and she always retained afterwards the painful sensation of their wounds.

Years later a similar incident took place at Pisa during one of Catherine's long ecstasies. As she told her confessor: "I saw the Lord, nailed to the cross, descend toward me in the midst of a brilliant light. . . . I saw five streams of blood issuing from the five wounds of the Savior and they were directed to the hands and feet and heart of my body. Realizing the significance of the vision, I cried out: Lord, at least grant that these wounds may remain invisible. Immediately the five streams of blood became five rays of light."

The incidents we have described suffice to show how Catherine had grown in her resemblance to our Lord, submitting faithfully and generously to His Will and not ceasing in her efforts to draw near to Him who had chosen her for His spouse. Gradually, through the purification of her senses and will, Catherine cleared the path of perfection which leads directly to the perfect contemplation that God gives to the clean of heart. The time was drawing near when Catherine's purity of heart was so great that she could say, in speaking of her love of God and of neighbor, that it was no longer she who loved but Jesus who loved in her. In proof of this statement, we shall cite one incident in her life of union with God. This incident is so marked with lyric poetry and profound spiritual significance that of itself it is sufficient to explain why Catherine rose to such heights of contemplation and rushed forth to the conquest of souls simply by letting her mouth speak from the fullness of her heart.

One day, Raymond tells us, after the departure of the other *Mantellate,* Catherine remained in prayer in the chapel of the Dominican church at Siena, the customary meeting place of the Sisters of Penance of St. Dominic. When she finally roused herself from her ecstasy in order to return home, she was enveloped by a light that descended from heaven. In the midst of the light the Savior appeared, holding in His sacred hands a human heart, red and glowing. Several days before, in a similar vision, Catherine had had the sensation that Jesus had taken her heart from her body. This day He gave her His heart in exchange, assuring her that He would give her eternal life.

Once again Raymond affirms that he had received this information from Catherine herself. But what interests us most in this incident is its deep symbolism. After this ineffable vision, Catherine's love of Jesus was so pure and disinterested that it can truly be said that it was Jesus who loved in her. Henceforth she would love all that Jesus loved —God above all and her neighbor for love of God. Through Jesus, she adored the Father who sent Him, the Word of which He is the incarnation, and the Holy Ghost who is eternally one with Them. With all the intensity of her love, Catherine was thenceforth united with the Three Persons in a contemplation that was increasingly more perfect.

Her vision of love broadened and deepened until her soul was transformed in God. She saw other creatures and herself in God and only in God did she consider herself and others. Completely docile to the divine inspirations, her soul was a living organ played by the Holy Ghost, who worked in her through His gifts—those gifts which, under the powerful breath of divine love in contemplation, illumine the obscure night of our intellect with flashes of lightning to strengthen the certainty of faith and, in the domain of action, show the road to be followed, lighting each step for the traveler and sustaining him in the struggle for divine life. A day would come, and it was already near, when Catherine's contemplation would be so permanent and her possession of God through love would be so complete and radiant that Jesus Himself would invite her to leave her cell and mingle with the world to live simultaneously the active and the contemplative life, thus fulfilling the letter and spirit of her father Dominic and her vocation as a Dominican: to give to others the fruits of contemplation.

There is one incident in Catherine's life which we have

purposely kept until now, because it seems to be a better summary and symbol than anything we could say to close this chapter. We are referring to her mystical marriage with Jesus.

For a long time, in imitation of His disciples, Catherine had begged our Lord to give her a great faith, a faith so solid that no opposing force could crush it or overwhelm it. She would then hear in her heart the answer of the Lord: "I shall espouse you in the faith." The day came when Jesus deigned to fulfill His promise. It was Shrove Tuesday, a day devoted to pleasure by worldlings, but to penance by Catherine. On this day the Lord appeared to her and said: "As I have promised you, I wish to espouse you in the faith." The Lord was still speaking when the Blessed Mother, St. John the Evangelist, the glorious Apostle Paul, St. Dominic, and the prophet David, with a harp in his hand, appeared. While the harp resounded with a sweetness surpassing all description under the fingers of the holy king, the Mother of God took the hand of Catherine and held the fingers out to her divine Son, asking Him whether He would consent to espouse Catherine in the faith. With a gracious sign of assent the Son of God took a golden ring set with four pearls and a diamond of incomparable beauty. With His right hand He put the band on the third finger of Catherine's hand and said: "I, your Creator and your Savior, espouse you in a faith you will preserve without any taint, until the day when you will celebrate with Me in heaven your eternal nuptials. Courage, my daughter, do manfully and without hesitation the works that the Order of My providence will place in your hands. Because you are ornamented with the power of faith, you will triumph over all your adversaries."

There is nothing to be added to such a message. One can expect everything of the apostolate of a soul who, as the spouse of Christ, is one with Him and, through Him, with God. From the heights of contemplation in which it has its source, the river of Catherine's love will spread out across a world of desolate souls and will bring a reflowering of faith and of love.

CHAPTER 5 🖎

The Apostolate

ALL the biographers of St. Catherine are in agreement in acknowledging the amplitude and efficacy of her apostolate. They disagree only when they attempt to determine the true causes of her apostolate. Those who reject a priori every explanation of a supernatural kind, under the pretext that the supernatural is beyond the scope of the biographer, try to explain Catherine's extraordinary apostolate by having recourse only to her natural qualities of mind and heart. But such explanations are out of harmony with the established facts. We willingly concede that Catherine was a highly intelligent woman, although uneducated; that she had an acute sagacity; that she was instinctively a diplomat, gifted with a true political sense; that on every occasion she manifested an indomitable will; and that she had a compassionate heart, quick to give itself and easily moved by the miseries of others. We even admit that the ensemble of these natural gifts contributed to some extent to the success of her apostolate.

But when one recalls the enormity and variety of the temporal and spiritual needs of her time that she had to meet, and when one analyzes the method of her apostolate —the way in which she took care of bodily and spiritual needs and the divine sources from which she invariably received and renewed the grace and strength that she lavished on all—it seems truly impossible to explain the extraordinary influence she exercised around her by having recourse merely to her natural gifts. Such purely natural qualities will never suffice to explain the power she had over the hearts most opposed to divine grace or her ability to soften the most hardened hearts, to convert wills most set in evil, to calm the most fiery temperaments, to cure souls through bodies, to expose herself without danger to the nursing of the most contagious diseases, and many other deeds even more astounding.

If Catherine had possessed only those qualities, even to the highest degree, undoubtedly she would not have passed unnoticed by her contemporaries. But her apostolate would certainly not have had the breadth or renown that even in our day calls forth the admiration of the world precisely because the sources that nourished it were not of this world. It is too often forgotten that Catherine was above all else a saint, an exceptional saint who, as a true daughter of Dominic, knew how to harmonize the active and the contemplative life and to find in her contemplation the very secret of her action.

Raymond of Capua describes how Catherine was invited by our Lord Himself to leave her interior cell in order to lead the active life. The account is of great interest to all, because it clarifies in a marvelous manner the way in which a Friar Preacher, if he is to remain faithful to the spirit of St. Dominic, must find in his contemplation a means of nourishing his activity and of making it fruitful.

"After the espousals," says Raymond, "the Lord began to draw His spouse into contact with society, but gradually, moderately, and in proportion to the need for this return. But He did not on that account take away from Catherine all the divine intimacies; in fact, He even made them more perfect, by giving them new depth.

"At first this invitation to leave her interior cell troubled Catherine. 'You know well,' she said to God, 'that I have fled from society in order to find You. Now that I have found You, thanks to Your mercy, and now that You have given me the happiness of possessing You, I ought never to abandon such an incomparable treasure to entangle myself again with human affairs. Once again my ignorance would increase and by letting myself go little by little, I would finally deserve Your reprobation. Never, Lord, never will your infinite goodness, in its limitless perfection, command me or others to do what could separate our souls from You.'"

How well we understand this objection of Catherine. She does not actually refuse to collaborate with Jesus in the salvation of souls, but she fears that a renewed contact with a world she had left long ago in order to find God may make her lose Him again. "Offer no resistance, My daughter," the Lord answered her. "It is thus that you must fulfill the commandment and allow My grace to bear fruit, not only in you but in others. I have no intention of separating you from Me in any way whatever, but I wish to use the love of neighbor to unite you more closely to Me. You know that My commandment of love is twofold: love of Me and love of neighbor. In this double commandment are contained the law and the prophets.[1] I wish you to fulfill these two precepts so that you will not walk with one foot, but with two; so that you will have two wings to fly to heaven. Remember that since your childhood, zeal for the salvation of souls has grown in your heart. It is I who have planted it there and have watered it. This zeal was such that you once thought of disguising yourself as a man in order to go to a country

[1] Matt. 22:40.

where you were unknown and enter the Order of Preachers, where you would better be able to help souls. If you so greatly desired the habit you are now wearing, it is because you had a special love for My faithful servant, Dominic, who founded his Order especially for the salvation of souls. Why, then, are you surprised and why do you complain of I lead you to a task that you have desired from your earliest youth?"

Comforted by these words, Catherine asked the Lord how that would be possible. "As My goodness disposes," He answered. The conversation continues but we shall not quote it here in its entirety. However, we cannot pass over in silence the reason the Lord Himself gave for choosing Catherine to preach the truth to the souls of her time. Catherine had said to Him: "Amen, may Your will be done, Lord. But what authority has a poor woman like me with men if I presume to preach the truth to them? They will make fun of me and will not listen to me. . . . 'It is not lack of faith that causes you to speak that way,' the Lord answered, 'but your humility. Then listen well. Am I not He who created the human race and formed both one and the other sex? Do I not give the grace of the Holy Ghost where I please? For Me there is no distinction between men and women, peasants and nobles. All are equal before Me, for My power reaches all equally.

" 'And here is the reason why I have chose you in particular. In these days there is such an excess of pride, especially among those who think themselves educated and wise, that My justice can wait no longer to confound them with a just judgment. But because My mercy always rules over My deeds, I am going to begin by inflicting on these proud ones a confusion that will be salutary and useful for them, if they will humble themselves by entering into themselves. . . . To confound their rashness I shall raise up women, ignorant and weak by nature, on whom I shall bestow heavenly wisdom and power. If they then humble themselves and acknowledge their guilt, I shall grant them My most plentiful mercies. . . . You will obey without hesitation when I decree to send you to the people. I shall not abandon you, no matter where you are. I shall not cease, for all that, to come to you as before and I shall direct you in all the things you will have to accomplish.' "

Several high points stand out in this touching conversation to help us understand Catherine's apostolate and grasp better the secret of her apostolic ministry. It was the Lord Himself who, from her childhood, had placed in Catherine's heart a zeal for the salvation of souls. It was He who had caused her to enter the Dominican Order, whose official mission in the Church is to work for the salvation of souls. Again, it was He who, with deliberate purpose, chose her, an illiterate woman, to humiliate the educated and the wise whose pride had drawn them far from God and to lead them to repentance. Lastly, it was He who, in order to help Catherine carry out this difficult mission, endowed her with heavenly wisdom and power.

Catherine's vocation was an exceptional vocation. It was entrusted to her by God in view of the needs peculiar to the souls of her day, whom pride had turned away in great numbers from the path of truth. And the success of this apostolate can be explained only by the heavenly wisdom and power with which God had favored her and the personal help He gave her in all the works she had to accomplish.

FIELD OF THE APOSTOLATE

Let us recall briefly what we have already said about the condition of society in Italy during the second half of the fourteenth century. Men in those days were no better than they are today. Instead of living in peace, they waged wars. In Siena, as from one end of the Italian peninsula to the other, factions triumphed and sacrificed the common good of a city or a province to the selfish interests of small groups or classes of citizens. The feud between the Guelphs and the Ghibellines was especially bitter and bloody. Not only individuals, but whole families—some of them the oldest and most honorable—rose up against each other and drowned their quarrels in blood. Violence triumphed over all other feelings and passion ruled over justice. In the eyes of authority mere suspicion was sufficient for arrest and condemnation. The prisons overflowed with political prisoners; hospitals, with the sick and wounded; and cities, with the poor. For, in addition to the political upheavals, a plague scourged Italy. Within a few days, two-thirds of the population of Siena had perished. After the plague, the famine ravaged many areas and bands of mercenary troops traveled around the country making raids on the helpless citizenry.

That is not all. To political dessensions, which generated hatred and discord, were added religious dissensions. It is the epoch in which the popes, ostensibly to flee from political factions and tyranny, left Rome to establish the papacy in Avignon, where they lived more or less under the yoke of the French. It was a fall from Charybdis to Scylla. Without a head, the Church in Italy collapsed into convulsions, to the great detriment of the clergy, both diocesan and religious, whose morals had already for some time left much to be desired. Catherine herself sketched a vivid and somber portrait of the sad condition of the clergy. We refer the reader to the second part of her *Dialogue*.

However, the morals of the laity were likewise correspondingly low. War, foreign or civil, has never been favorable for good morals, no more than have plague and famine. The real victims of these three scourges are not the ones who succumb in body, but those who escape with their lives and then, as a reaction to so many trials, wallow in pleasures of all kinds.

The relaxation of morals in Italy coincides with the rise of the Renaissance, whose pagan spirit inaugurated a new era of independence in regard to authority of every kind, political, moral, or religious. Wherever it breathed on souls, individualism blossomed forth. Our Lord referred to this in particular when He spoke to Catherine of the pride of the educated and the wise whom He wished to humble by having a woman preach the gospel to them. Nevertheless, He does not condemn knowledge, but the abuse they had made of it in order to cut themselves off from religion and to draw in their wake the ignorant masses. "Knowledge in itself is good and perfect," He said to Catherine in the *Dialogue,* "when a learned person is also good, honorable, and humble in life. But if knowledge be joined with a proud, dishonorable, and wicked life, it is a poison." [2]

This panorama of the morals of society in the time of St. Catherine is rather somber and one can easily understand why a contemplative would hesitate to leave the company of saints and of God to mingle with the proud, the depraved, and the free-thinkers. Nevertheless, it is well to note that at this time, around the middle of the fourteenth century, it was not so much the faith that was in danger in Italy, but morals. The faith was menaced from without by the ever-present possibility of invasion by the infidels who still held the Holy Land, but inside Italy it was not yet the object of any direct attack; at least there was no concerted attack. From one end of Italy to the other, people continued to believe, to crowd the churches, and to multiply devotions. But

[2] *Dialogue,* Chap. CXXVII.

under all the influences we have just mentioned, the aristocrats, the bourgeois, and the artisans were trying to reconcile Christian thought with a pagan life. They lacked love
more than faith. They believed in God but they did not love
Him, at least not in the profound sense in which God wishes
to be loved—for Himself and above all things. Nor did their
love of God lead to the love of neighbor as one's self through
the whole-hearted and daily practice of the Christian virtues.

Under conditions such as these it must be recognized that
no one was better prepared than Catherine to preach the
gospel to her contemporaries, to spread among them her doctrine of love, to denounce their pride, self-love, and sensuality, and to scourge their hatred of their brothers, their in-
human violence, and their social injustices. Although
Catherine had withdrawn from the world since the age of
seven and had lived the greater part of her life in her interior
cell, she was not ignorant of the lamentable condition of the
world of her day nor of the mortal danger that souls were
encountering in it. Her brothers in St. Dominic had surely
not neglected to inform her on this topic, but in reading the
Dialogue one sees that God took it upon Himself to make
these things known to her and to keep her informed on
everything it was important for her to know in view of her
apostolate.

Three ideas gradually became dominant in her mind as
she grew to realize the difficulties to be overcome and the
needs to be met in her apostolate. First, there was need of a
general reform in the morals of the clergy, both diocesan and
religious, from the lowliest priest to the highest prelate;
secondly, a Crusade would have to be organized to drive the
infidels from the Holy Land; and lastly, the Pope must return to Rome. This last project, she thought, would bring
peace to Italy and to the Church. But while these ideas were

maturing in her mind and as she waited for the opportunity to put them into execution, Catherine attended to other urgent and pressing problems. She began to exercise a personal apostolate among the poor, the sick, and the prisoners.

CARE OF THE POOR

What Catherine saw above all in the poor was that they were her brothers, the suffering members of the great human family whose common Father is God. The sight of their wretchedness filled her heart with pity. She did not wait until they begged alms from her before she went to their aid. It was enough for her to know that they were in real need. Personally she had nothing to give them, but her father had given permission, as Raymond of Capua tells us, for her to dispense his goods as she wished among the poor. He had likewise notified the rest of the household to allow her to do so.

In Catherine's eyes the poor were not only her brothers in a common humanity, but she saw Jesus Christ in them. While giving them alms, she showed them respect and affection, as if they had been the Son of God Himself. To assure her that she was not deceiving herself and to encourage her in her practices of charity, Jesus often appeared to her as one of the poor, the tattered, or the starving. The famous miracle of the chapel of the *Mantellate* is a case in point.

One day when the Dominican friars had just chanted Tierce and the faithful had withdrawn, Catherine remained with a companion to pray in the chapel which adjoined the nave of the church. Just as she was descending from the chapel into the body of the church, the Lord appeared to her under the appearance of a traveler of about thirty years of age, poor and almost naked. He asked Catherine to take pity on him in the name of God and to give him some clothing. "Wait a moment, my brother," Catherine said to him, "until I go back into the chapel and I will give you some clothing." She went back up the steps to the chapel and, with the help of her companion, she removed a sleeveless woolen tunic she was wearing under her tertiary habit. Returning to the church, she gave it to the poor vagabond.

But the beggar did not appear satisfied. After receiving the woolen tunic, he asked for a linen tunic with sleeves. "In that case," said Catherine, "follow me home." There Catherine gave him everything that he requested and Raymond lets us know that there seemed to be no end to his demands, first for himself and then for one of his friends in the hospital. Finally, Catherine had nothing more to give and she wondered whether she ought not give him the very tunic she was wearing. But Raymond tells us that her modesty mastered her charity. God had taught her that one could not offend against one virtue in order to practice another; discretion forbade it. To her intense regret, Catherine apologized to the beggar, saying she was now poorer than he.

The following night Jesus again appeared to her in the guise of the same beggar, holding in His hands the famous sleeveless tunic. "My daughter," He said, "yesterday you gave Me this tunic with such liberality and you showed such love in clothing My nakedness to protect Me from shame and the cold that I am going to give you in exchange an invisible garment which will protect your body and soul from all cold until that day when you will be clothed with glory and honor before the angels and saints."

We have related this miracle of Catherine's charity because it so clearly portrays the spontaneity of her charity, her prodigality in stripping herself of possessions, and her prudence in the gift of herself. These are characteristic of her manner of acting and we shall find them even more evident in her apostolate properly so-called, when she will no longer be aiding only the bodies of men, but their souls.

NURSING THE SICK

In addition to the poor, and for more numerous reasons, Catherine was attracted to the sick. She who endured suffering so courageously, could not bear to see others suffer, especially when their suffering separated them from God instead of drawing them nearer to Him. Catherine, today the patroness of nurses,[3] hovered lovingly around the beds of the sick and in certain instances carried her devotion to the point of heroism. For example, one cannot read the account of the cure and conversion of Andrea without trembling before a spectacle which surpasses the expectations of human nature and disconcerts the most intrepid wills and most generous hearts.

Andrea was, like Catherine, a Sister of Penance of St. Dominic, a *Mantellata,* but widowed and already aged. She suffered from a cancer of the breast which was spreading over the entire chest and gave off an unbearable odor. Catherine took upon herself the care of Andrea and performed her duties with all the ardor of her charity. One day, when physical disgust rose up while she was caring for the poor sick woman, she pressed her lips to the horrible wound until she gained her self-control. The sick woman marveled at such courage. Nevertheless, little by little, under the influence of the devil, whom such an act disturbed, she began to suspect Catherine's intentions, then to hate her, and finally to defame her and accuse her of evil conduct during the hours when she was not with her.

[3] Cf. *Inter Gravissimas,* September 15, 1943, *Acta Apostolica Sedis,* XXXVI, p. 68.

When the accusation reached the ears of the other *Mantellate,* they became alarmed and the Prioress summoned Catherine and demanded an explanation. To all the accusations brought against her virtue and her honor, Catherine answered calmly: "In truth, my Sisters, I am a virgin."

When Lapa learned of the infamy, she demanded that her daughter leave the service of the old woman who had maligned her. But as always, Catherine turned to our Lord and put her case in His hands. At this point in the affair, Jesus appeared to Catherine, as we have already described, and gave her the choice of a jeweled diadem or a crown of thorns. Catherine chose the crown of thorns. Then Jesus said to her: "Persevere in the service you have undertaken and I will give you complete victory over the evil one."

Comforted by this promise, Catherine returned to her patient and cared for her with the same devotion as if nothing had happened between them. Andrea was overcome by Catherine's humility and charity and had to admit that she was vanquished. One day, when her bed was bathed in light at the coming of Catherine, she looked up and saw Catherine's face transfigured. Immediately she broke into sobs, asked pardon of her saintly nurse for having so deeply offended her, and would not cease until she had repaired her fault and proclaimed the sanctity of Catherine.

Indifferent to the restoration of her good name, Catherine continued to nurse Andrea with loving care. In fact, her devotedness seemed to increase as the disease grew more serious and repulsive. Mistress of herself and completely given over to her apostolate for the love of God and the soul she wished to win for Him, Catherine succeeded so well in overcoming her sensibilities that she no longer felt any disgust when caring for the poor sick woman whose flesh was falling into decay. On one occasion she went so far as to drink without flinching, as if it were a glass of water, the bowl of liquid with which she had just washed Andrea's festering wound.

Raymond is not alone in recounting this incident. We also find an account of it in the testimony of Bartholomew Dominici. The incident seemed so extraordinary to Raymond that he felt more than ever the need to quote witnesses. "I gathered all these facts from Catherine in her personal confessions," he states, "and I also found them in the writings of Brother Thomas, her first confessor, in the accounts of the brethren of my Order, and in those of other trustworthy people, such as Catherine's companions, whose names I am prepared to repeat, if necessary, since I have already given them in other instances."

SOLACE FOR PRISONERS

Although the poor and the sick absorbed the greater part of her time, Catherine also occupied herself with the prisoners of Siena. We have a beautiful letter, dated April 9, 1377, and addressed to the Sienese prisoners whom she greeted as "My dear sons in Christ, the sweet Jesus." The purpose of this letter is clear: to urge these unfortunate persons to be patient and to invite them to receive the sacraments at Easter. Catherine makes no direct reference to their sufferings in prison nor to the reasons, just or unjust, of their imprisonment. That was a delicate subject and she would be in danger of injustice toward the prisoners or the authorities who had sentenced them. She takes up the most important problem, that of sin in general, whose prisoners we all are and from which Jesus delivered us by dying on the cross for love of us.

"He bore pain, calumny, mistreatment, and outrages; He was bound, scourged, and nailed to the cross; He was covered with insults and injuries and tormented by thirst. But He suffered everything with patience, forgiving and praying for those who crucified Him." [4] The lesson is clear, but how delicately it is presented. Jesus was innocent. It is for us, for our sins, that He endured all this pain with divine patience. After such an example, how can we complain, we who are not free from sin? "He was a knight fighting on the battlefield. . . . His crown of thorns was His helmet; His lacerated flesh, . . . His armor; the nails in His hands, His gauntlets; the lance in His side, His sword; and the nails in His feet, His spurs. See how well-armed is our Knight. We ought to follow Him and look to Him for all consolation in our trials and tribulations." [5]

But Catherine was not content to write beautiful and consoling letters to the prisoners. When the time came for one of them to pay with his life for his crimes—or what was quite common in that day, for his political indiscretions—she would go to him and console him in his last moments, hoping at least to snatch his soul from eternal death. Such was the case of young Nicholas di Tuldo, who had been condemned to death for a trifling thing—a few thoughtless words spoken out of bravado when under the influence of wine at a banquet. The details of the condemnation of Nicholas, his revolt against society and against God, whose name he did not even wish to hear mentioned by any priest or religious, his conversion and edifying death, are known from Catherine's magnificent letter to Raymond of Capua. It is one of the most beautiful of all the letters preserved by Catherine's disciples.

"I went to visit him whom you know and it gave him so much comfort and joy that he made his confession and prepared himself well. He entreated me for the love of God to

[4] Letter 260.   [5] *Ibid.*

promise that I would be with him when the hour of execution came. I gave him my word and kept it. And in the morning, before the first stroke of the bell, I went to him and he was greatly consoled. I took him to hear Mass and he received Holy Communion, to which he had always been disinclined. His will was united to the will of God and submissive to it, but he was afraid of not being strong enough at the decisive moment. . . . And he said: 'Stay with me and do not leave me. Then all will be well and I shall die content.' Then he rested his head upon my breast and I felt a great exultation and perceived the fragrance of his blood as though it had blended with the fragrance of my own blood, which I desire to shed for my sweet Spouse Jesus. This desire grew in my soul, and because I perceived how great was his anguish, I murmured: 'Have courage, brother, for soon we shall be at the eternal marriage feast. You shall go forth bathed in the sweet blood of the Son of God, with the sweet name of Jesus, which must never pass from your memory, and I shall await you at the place of execution.' O my father and my son, all fear then vanished from his heart and the sorrow on his face was transformed into joy. In his happiness he said to me: 'Whence comes so great a grace that the sweetness of my soul awaits me at the holy place of execution?' See what light he had received, that he could call the place of execution holy! He then added: 'Yes, I shall go forth joyfully, and when I think that you will await me there, it seems to me that I have yet a thousand years to wait.' And he spoke such sweet words that it seemed my heart would break because God is so good.

"I waited for him at the place of execution, praying and invoking unceasingly the assistance of Mary and of Catherine, virgin and martyr. Before his arrival I lay down and placed my neck on the block but without obtaining that which I desired. I prayed and stormed heaven, saying 'Mary!' I wanted to obtain the grace that she would gain light and peace for him in his last moments. My soul was so inebriated with the promise that I had received that I did not see any-one, although there was a great crowd in the square.

"Then he came, gentle as a lamb, and when he saw me he began to smile. He wanted me to make the sign of the cross over him. When I had done so, I said to him in a low voice: 'Go my dear brother; soon you shall be at the eternal marriage feast.' With great meekness he lay down and I bared his neck. Then, bending down to him, I reminded him of the blood of the Lamb. His lips said nothing but 'Jesus' and 'Catherine.' I closed my eyes, saying: 'I will,' and received his head in my hands.

"Then I saw the God-Man, and His brightness was like that of the sun. . . . This soul entered into the open wound in His side, and Truth made me understand that this soul was saved by pure grace and mercy, without any merit on his part.

"And that soul then did something that was so sweet that a thousand hearts could not contain it. . . . It had already begun to taste the divine sweetness when it turned around, as the bride turns at the bridegroom's door and, looking back, bows her head in farewell and thanksgiving to those who have attended her." [6]

Such are, among many others, some of the most beautiful traits of Catherine's apostolate of charity among the poor, the sick, and the prisoners. One can see that for her, love of one's neighbor is no idle word. As soon as anyone comes to seek her aid, even materially, she is ready to do anything, even at the risk of her life. As a true daughter of St. Dominic,

[6] Letter 273.

who sold his books to get money for the poor, Catherine was ingenious in finding ways to assist them. But in her eyes, as in the eyes of St. Dominic, the truly poor were the sinners and the thousands of souls who did not know God, or knew Him but slightly, or foolishly preferred their small wisdom to the wisdom and love of God. She was seized with a great pity for them and wished to preach the truth to them and open her heart to them. For what other reason had she entered the Order of Friars Preachers and for what other purpose had God Himself revealed to her His doctrine of love? The most perfect alms, she would say, is the alms of truth. The office of St. Dominic, as the Lord told her, "was that of My only-begotten Son, the Word. Rightly he appeared in the world as an apostle and sowed the seed of My Word with much truth and light, dissipating darkness and giving light." [7]

But the same mission which God had previously confided to Dominic, when the Albigensians were poisoning the whole of southern France and northern Italy with their heresies, He likewise entrusted to Catherine a century later. "I have chosen you in particular to preach My truth to the souls of these times, in order to confound the pride of those who think themselves educated and wise and to lead them to repentance. . . . That is why I have endowed you with divine wisdom and power."

Catherine's apostolate was first of all doctrinal, as that of every Dominican ought to be. God revealed His doctrine of love, as she recorded it in the *Dialogue,* only that she might teach it to her contemporaries, after she herself had completely assimilated it in the light and fire of contemplation.

And that is what she did from the day that the Lord commanded her, as He had commanded the apostles and her

[7] *Dialogue,* Chap. CXXXIX.

brethren in St. Dominic, to preach His truth to souls and for their sake to unite the active and the contemplative life. Catherine, of course, could not ascend to the pulpit and preach to large congregations. It is not the role of women to preach thus. Nevertheless, by words in her conversations and private conferences and by pen in her letters she exercised a magnificent teaching apostolate, the echoes of which still reverberate in our day. We must speak of this oral and written apostolate and, as far as is possible after five centuries, try to revive her flaming eloquence.

THE ELOQUENCE OF LOVE

Following the most extraordinary vision she had ever had of God, which she recounted to Raymond of Capua under obedience, Catherine declared that after such happiness she suffered impatience at being held in the prison of her body. "If I were not bound by the love of God and neighbor, for which reason God sent me back to my body, I would die of longing."

While seeing God in the vision, she was able to form some idea of the glory of the saints and the torments of sinners. Jesus had said to her: "You see with what pains those who offend Me are punished. Return to them to show them their error, their danger, and the wrong they do Me."

"My soul," says Catherine, "was seized with a mortal fear of returning to the world. But the Lord said to me: 'The souls of many depend upon your return. . . . It will even be necessary, for the salvation of souls, that you leave the city of your birth. But I shall be with you always, and I shall lead you forth and bring you back again. You will carry the honor of My name to the lowly and the great, to the laity as well as to the religious and clergy. I shall give you an eloquence and a wisdom that no one will be able to resist.

I shall send you to pontiffs, to those who govern the Church and the Christian people, for, as is My custom, I shall confound the pride of the strong with one who is weak.' "

At the recollection of this vision, which could almost be called beatific (Catherine told Raymond that he could be certain that her soul had beheld the divine essence), Catherine could not restrain her tears. "This is not surprising, Father, but what is truly surprising is that my heart does not break anew each day that I think of the glory I possessed at that moment and which today, alas, is far removed from me. It is the salvation of souls which is the cause of all that. Therefore, who would be amazed that I love so dearly those whom the All-high has charged me to warn and convert from evil to good. They have cost me a great deal, for because of them I have become anathema to the Lord, and the joy of His glory has been postponed to a time that I do not yet know. That is why, as St. Paul says, these faithful are my glory, my crown, and my joy.[8] I tell you these things so that your heart may not share the pain of those who murmur against me when they see that I have become the servant of all."

The successes of Catherine's apostolate, as recounted by her disciples and biographers, surpassed in number and quality all that her exceptional vocation would have enabled them to foresee. When a sinner fell into her hands, one could be almost certain he would be converted. Her power of attraction was irresistible. Crowds came to hear her, and both those who were brought to her by force and those whom she met unexpectedly were equally enthusiastic once they had heard her.

Bartholomew Dominici, who had been her disciple for about fifteen years and knew her well, tells us that "like a

[8] Cf. Phil. 4:1.

burning seraphim, she quickly aroused the fear and love of God in those who were touched by her words of instruction. What is astonishing is that ordinarily the more educated the persons whom she addressed, the more quickly they responded with admiration and devotion. Under the impetus of divine grace, so great was her eloquence in her exhortations that women and men formed in crowds to hear the words that fell from her lips." Bartholomew remarked elsewhere that it was enough to be near her to feel better. Although young and of a pleasing countenance, she impressed people immediately by the radiance of her virtue and especially by her purity. The power of her words increased ten-fold because of this.

How one wishes that he could have heard her! Her disciples and her biographers agree that those who had this opportunity were for the most part unable to resist her attraction. Whether they were converted or did not need conversion, their lives were improved. She had a way of speaking of God, of Jesus Christ and His love for men, of ungrateful men, of the horror of sin, of the cross and the blood of Jesus Christ, the sweet Savior, that stirred her listeners profoundly and inspired them to make manly resolutions.

It was in this way that she converted the heart of Nicholas di Saraceni, a Sienese soldier who had spent his life as a mercenary in the service of different factions and parties. When he finally returned to his home, he spent his time administering his goods and feasting with his townsmen. He looked forward to a long and comfortable life. Urged by his wife and several members of his family to see Catherine, he promised to do so. But it was only after he had had a dream about her and was curious to see whether the reality corresponded with the dream that he actually went to see her.

The reality must have far supassed his dream, for after

listening to Catherine, the soldier was so deeply moved that he was speechless. He confessed his sins to Thomas della Fonte and even went back to the confessional a second time in order to confess a sin which he had forgotten and of which Catherine reminded him.

What she achieved with Nicholas di Saraceni, she also achieved with the Tolomei family and with Andrew di Naddino, an impenitent sinner who, up to his last moments, would not hear of confession and did nothing but blaspheme. He was finally converted because Catherine, who had heard of the case from her confessor, Thomas della Fonte, undertook to obtain Andrew's pardon from God. She pleaded with such eloquent fervor that the Lord relented and, in a moment, turned the heart of the unfortunate man. Andrew asked for the priest and with great sorrow accused himself of the sins of his whole life.

We could multiply examples like this indefinitely but we shall be content to relate one incident which summarizes all the others and reveals Catherine's method of procedure when the conversion of a sinner was at stake. We refer to the famous Nannes of Siena who, as Raymond tells us, promoted and incited personal feuds or vendettas against many of his fellow citizens, as was too often done in those times. He prepared secret ambushes against them, all the while pretending to be going innocently about his affairs. On many occasions he was connected with the murder of a man but in such a secret way that the actual executioners of the deed feared Nannes more than the vengeance of their victims, for they knew his craftiness. Mediators had often interposed to urge him to make peace, but the clever Nannes always answered by saying that this affair did not concern him and that peace did not depend on him. Yet all the while he alone was putting obstacles in the way of peace in order to get his revenge as he pleased.

When she learned of the state of affairs, Catherine eagerly desired to speak to Nannes, but he fled from her like the serpent flees from the charmer. He finally consented to meet her, but with the firm intention of not following her advice. He went to see her, but she was not at home. As he was about to leave, Catherine returned unexpectedly. Then began a bitter struggle and the victory would go to the keener of the two. Nannes finally made a concession by saying he would give up one feud out of four. Catherine gave him to understand that that was not the way to act and that in the name of God she demanded all or nothing. When he still resisted, she spoke to God directly. While she was praying, her confessor tried to hold Nannes back when he showed by his expression that he wished to depart. He was already getting up to leave, when suddenly he cried out: "Oh, God, what consolation I feel in my soul for that single word of peace: that I would give up one out of four!" Then he added: "Oh, Lord God, what force holds me back? I cannot leave and I cannot refuse anything! Who is restraining me? Who holds me captive?" And while he was speaking, he burst into tears. "I confess that I am defeated," he said, "I can no longer breathe." Then he fell to his knees and, weeping, he said: "O holy virgin, I shall do all that you command, not only for the peace but in regard to everything else. I think the devil had me in chains, but now I wish to follow your advice. Tell me how I can free my soul from the hands of the demon."

If we accept the testimony of Raymond of Capua and Bartholomew Dominici, the conversions effected by Catherine's inflamed eloquence and ardent prayer must be counted by the thousands. And these two witnesses cannot be accused of exaggeration because they offer official documents to substantiate their statements. "Who could count the criminals," Raymond asks, "whom she snatched from the gates of hell, the hardened sinners she brought to realize their state, the worldings she led to despise the world, the souls afflicted by temptations whom she delivered from the snare of the devil by her prayers and teachings, the elect whom she directed in the paths of virtue, the holy souls whom she urged to the pursuit of perfection, and the unfortunate ones she saved from the degradation of their sins? She sustained these unhappy ones by suffering for them and praying for them. One could almost say that she carried them on her own shoulders along the path of truth and that she led them to the gates of eternal life.

"At times my own eyes have seen a thousand or more people, both men and women, as at the call of an invisible trumpet, hasten from the mountains and other regions around Siena to see and hear the saint. Not only her words, but merely the sight of her was sometimes enough to make them repent of their crimes. They wept, they moaned over their sins, and flocked to the confessors. I was one of these confessors and I found such a lively contrition in these penitents that no one could doubt that a shower of grace had descended from heaven into their hearts. And that happened not only once or twice, but very often. The Sovereign Pontiff, Gregory XI, of happy memory, rejoicing in all the good that was being done for souls gave to my companions and myself special apostolic letters which conferred on us powers equal to those of a diocesan bishop. We were empowered to absolve all those who came to Catherine and asked to go to confession."

Bartholomew Dominici cites the bull of Gregory XI to

which Raymond alludes and in which the Pope gave Catherine permission to choose three confessors who would accompany her and absolve those she would send to them. The number of penitents was so great that Raymond admits, to his shame and Catherine's glory, that he was exhausted. But seeing the great joy of Catherine, which she could not help but manifest externally, he forgot his fatigue and rejoiced interiorly.

From the crowd of penitents who had been attracted by her words, Catherine had the satisfaction of seeing a certain number of men and women become her disciples. We have already named three principal ones, Stephen Maconi, Barduccio Camiggioni, and Neri Landucci. To these three she dictated her *Dialogue* toward the end of her life. But there were many others also to whom she dictated her letters. They never left her and they formed a kind of bodyguard always ready to defend her against her enemies. For this holy girl, so humble, so gentle, and so exclusively interested in doing penance, living in union with God and saving souls, was not loved and admired by all. She had implacable enemies even among the clergy and in her own Order. Jealous and envious, they cast suspicion on the orthodoxy of her teaching; they criticized her fasts and abstinences and her life of mortification, by which, they said, she wished to be singular and to make herself an example for others. These enemies ultimately denounced her to the Master General of the Order, Elias of Toulouse, and Catherine was summoned to the General Chapter of the Order, held in Florence in 1374. Fortunately, the accusations were proved to be false and the Chapter approved Catherine's teaching and life. She could then return to Siena and tranquilly resume her active and contemplative life.

Doubtless, at a distance of five centuries we cannot form

an exact idea of Catherine's preaching. It is the fate of eloquence to disappear with the orator, even to vanish with each discourse. An orator must be heard to be appreciated. Those who heard Catherine—Raymond, Bartholomew Dominici, her disciples, and admirers—have insisted that she captivated crowds and that one could not resist her colorful and flaming words. We are forced to accept their statements without being able to experience the reality.

Fortunately for us, Catherine not only spoke but she wrote. If we are unable to hear her, we can at least read her. Approximately four hundred of her letters have come down to us. It is regrettable that certain passages have been deleted, observations and practical details that would have given us much more information about the psychology of St. Catherine. They have, in fact, been so abridged that they contain nothing but what might edify. Nevertheless, such as they are, they not only corroborate what her contemporaries have told us of her eloquence, but they also give us exact information about her doctrine, her apostolate, and her apostolic method. In our eyes that is priceless, and the reading of her words consoles us for not having heard her.

CATHERINE'S LETTERS

Catherine would not have been a true daughter of St. Dominic if she had not been concerned about preaching to souls the marvelous doctrine of love that God Himself had revealed to her. One can be certain that in her oral preaching as well as in her letters she spoke of God, of Jesus Christ, of His ineffable love for sinners, the sufferings He endured for them, the blood He shed for their sake, the Church He founded, the sacraments He instituted, the faith we ought to have, the charity we ought to practice, the faults to be avoided, and the moral virtues to be acquired.

Her letters are filled with this doctrine of love, later con-signed to the *Dialogue*. Only the tone is different. Her let-ters are not, as is the *Dialogue*, simply a doctrinal exposition. They are the accents of a fiery soul who addresses herself personally to her correspondents and teaches them the doc-trine she had learned from God. But she teaches them only after long meditation on the doctrine and after it has passed, so to speak, through the fire of her contemplation. Actually, the letters were dictated by Catherine to her disciples in the midst of her numerous ecstasies when, in the presence of God and under the inspiration of the Holy Ghost, her faith and charity were enriched by those divine assurances and intuitions that are the privilege of contemplatives and the savory fruit of the gifts of knowledge, understanding, and wisdom.

Blessed were those disciples who, as they took her dicta-tion, could hear the words of fire fall from Catherine's lips, like burning lava erupting from a volcano. But in the writ-ing, these words have necessarily cooled. Now that we can no longer hear Catherine but must be content to read her words, we cannot picture the palpitation of the ecstatic soul whose mouth spoke out of the abundance of a heart that was one with the heart of God in the fullness of contemplation. However, at such times the feeling of her disciples was so intense that even under the cooled lava of the sentences they wrote, we sense the throbbing of Catherine's soul and the beating of her heart in her singularly personal manner of speaking, the warmth that flows through her sentences, the inimitable accent that punctuates certain cadences, and the rhythm that now rushes ahead or now slackens its speed.

Thanks to her letters, we can also form an accurate idea of Catherine's apostolic method and at the same time im-agine the fire of her preaching. One may say that hers is a method of authority in which, to make it more efficacious and more suitable to her correspondents, she unites all her natural and supernatural qualities of spirit and heart: on the one hand, her intrepid faith and ardent love, both enriched by the springs of her contemplation, and on the other hand, her acute intellect, her finesse of spirit as well as her spirit of finesse, her robust common sense, her strong will, her generous heart, and her quivering sensitivity. The whole ensemble was placed at the service of souls who had to be enlightened and inspired to win them for Jesus Christ.

When one reads the letters of Catherine superficially, especially if one reads them all in order, without taking the trouble to refer to the circumstances that motivated them and to the sort of people to whom they were written, one cannot escape a certain feeling of monotony. She preaches the same doctrine to all and, necessarily, she repeats. That is not her fault, but the fault of truth, which does not change. But if one wishes to take the time to identify her correspondents, to learn something about the persons to whom the letters were addressed, and why she was writing to them, then the view changes. She speaks to all with authority in the name of God and from a heart that floods over with love. Her language is always striking and rich in imagery; she goes straight to the point without any deviations. But she does not speak to all in the same tone nor in the same manner. With nuances of expression and feeling she adapts what she has to say and the way she will say it to each person. These nuances escape us if we are to read the letters without knowing to whom they are addressed, but they astonish those who do know, just as they must have greatly impressed the persons to whom they were written. We shall cite several types of letters so that the reader will comprehend the degree to which this daughter of St. Dominic knew how to preach truth to souls and with what psychology she adapted herself to her correspondents, without ever hurting anyone but never betraying truth.

In her letters to her mother, Catherine manifests a filial tenderness, but at the same time she is quick to vindicate her right to consecrate herself to the service of God and the salvation of souls. Her mother suffered because she did not always have Catherine near at hand and she sometimes reproached her for her repeated and prolonged absences. Gently, but tenderly and firmly, Catherine tried to make Lapa understand that this was not the right way to look at the matter.

"As a good and dear mother," she writes from Avignon, "you must be content and not desolate at my absence, for the honor of God and for your salvation and mine. Remember that when your sons went forth into the world for the sake of worldly gain you did not oppose them. Now, when for me it is a question of gaining eternal life, that seems to you to be too heavy a burden to bear and you even speak of dying if I do not write to you as soon as possible. All that comes from your loving that part of myself which I have from you, the flesh with which I am clothed, more than the soul that I have from God. Lift up your heart and affection to that most holy and sweet Cross which makes all fatigue more bearable; consent to bear a little suffering in order to avoid the infinite suffering we have merited because of our sins. May the love of Christ crucified comfort you. Do not believe yourself forsaken either by God or by me." [9]

Such letters, so rich in Christian doctrine and human tenderness, must have deeply touched the heart of Lapa. The daughter seems to be giving her mother a lesson, but the lesson is permeated with such delicacy of soul that the

[9] Letter 240.

mother cannot help but admit deep inside that her daughter was right.

With her spiritual father, Raymond of Capua, whose supernatural spirit and natural timidity she well knew, Catherine did not have to take such great care when she presumed to remind him of the doctrine of love and at the same time give him advice. Certainly she did not forget that she was his spiritual daughter, and in this regard she always showed great respect to him and was prompt in her obedience. But in another way, or more precisely, on another plane, Raymond was at the same time her spiritual son and she did not hesitate to speak authoritatively when the opportunity arose. The following letter throws light on the way Catherine acted.

"Dearest and sweetest Father and negligent and ungrateful son in the sweet Christ Jesus: I write to you in His precious blood in the desire of seeing you employ true and perfect eagerness in acquiring and preserving virtue, because without that eagerness the soul will never acquire virtue, and if it already possesses virtue, it will never preserve it. Love makes the heart industrious and urges it to go where virtue is to be found. If a soul does not have this industry, it is a sign that it does not love. It is proper that you should love manfully and unreservedly, not letting yourself be influenced by sensuality nor by anything else. But to attain such a love you must open the eye of your intellect and understand and see how much God loves us. That is to say, it is necessary to enter wholeheartedly into the cell of self-knowledge, where hatred of our own sensuality is engendered and love of God for His inestimable charity toward us is born. Then the heart is aroused under the incentive of inflamed desire and endeavors to find ways to use its time as perfectly as possible . . . and it perceives that to attain true virtue there is no other way than love of neighbor." [10]

But what fatigue that entails, and to bear this fatigue, what patience is needed! Fatigue is, for Catherine, the best word to describe what we call the burdens of life. By that term she means the sum total of the various trials that mark all our lives. "The repercussion of this fatigue is felt in the very depths of our soul. We sense that she knew well this fatigue, she who was so valiant and courageous. So often, with melancholy complacency, she names the various kinds of fatigue: weariness of body and soul, exhaustion from heavy tasks; weariness from impotent efforts; weariness from human injustice, lassitude from separation and heart-breaks, ennui from struggles and personal trials. But we must bear all fatigue manfully; we must bear it with a calm and tranquil soul. And that is the purpose of patience." [11]

Then, to encourage her spiritual father to devote his time to the service of his neighbor and to endure all the fatigue that accompanies the practice of fraternal charity, she began to praise the holy virtue of patience with a sincerity that was the fruit of her own experience, using a host of images that give her language great color and brillance:

"O patience, how lovable you are! O patience, what hope you give to him who possesses you! O patience, you are a queen who governs anger and is not dominated by it. O patience, you punish sensuality when it raises its head in anger. You have in your hand the two-edged sword that extirpates anger, pride, and that marrow of pride which is impatience! And these two edges are hatred and love. You are clothed like the sun, you are clothed in the light of true knowledge of God and of the fire of divine charity. You cast rays of light on those who insult you; you heap glowing coals of charity on

[10] Letter 104.   [11] Lemonnyer, *op. cit.,* p. 81.

their heads. The hatred in their hearts is burned and consumed. Yes, O sweet patience founded on charity, you bear fruit in the neighbor and give honor to God. Your robe is set with stars, which are the different virtues. In fact, patience cannot exist in the soul without the stars of all the virtues. Self-knowledge precedes patience like the light of the moon which illumines the night. Then comes daybreak, brightness, and heat, which is patience clothed like the sun. Who would not be enamored of this sweet patience! [12]

"Forward then, dearest and sweetest Father. Lose no time, but apply yourself to self-knowledge so that this queen may dwell in your soul. This is very necessary. Flee all conversation except that required for saving souls and snatching them out of the hands of the demon in holy confession. For that reason, be happy to be in the company of publicans and sinners. . . . Do not be slow and negligent when it is a question of praying to God and serving your neighbor." [13]

How evident it is from reading these passages that Catherine was consumed with zeal for the house of God. This alone explains the daring frankness with which she writes to her spiritual father and encourages him in the apostolate in such an importunate and personal way. Here also one obtains a keen insight into her apostolic method. We have called it a method of authority in our attempt to define it. In virtue of this authoritarianism in God's name, St. Catherine put into effect all her means of action, both natural and supernatural, and all her qualities of mind and heart for the salvation of souls, whether she wrote to them personally or whether she appealed to the conscience and zeal of those whose duty it was to work for the salvation of souls.

Whether it was a question of the needs of individual

[12] Letter 104.   [13] *Ibid.*

souls or those of society, such as the reform of the clergy, the freeing of the Holy Land, or the return of the popes from Avignon to Rome for the general good of Italy and the Church, Catherine always applied the same apostolic method: "I will, *Io voglio*," which in reality means: God wills it! Before all else, it is a question of giving to God what is due Him—honor and glory. But the honor and glory of God are intimately connected with the salvation of souls. In fact, He placed His glory in their salvation by giving them His only Son and by willing to be repaid by them with love. The apostolate, then, ought to consist in arousing in souls at every opportunity the love of God and all that it implies: horror of sin, the practice of all the virtues, humble and constant submission to His redemptive will in all personal and social circumstances, the worship and imitation of Jesus Christ, and loyalty and devotion to His Church and to His visible head, the sweet Christ on the earth.

In her letters, Catherine does nothing more than recall to each of her correspondents the immense love of God for men and the obligation of His creatures, whoever they may be, to love Him with all their hearts. Her whole doctrine consists in this, and in any exposition that she gives of it one senses an extraordinary apostolic breathing which never abates, the very breathing of the Holy Ghost who dwells in her soul and with whom she is always in contact. That is the primary reason for the efficacy of her apostolic method. Those to whom she wrote found it difficult to escape the breath of fire which still moves us today when we read her letters. Much less were they able to escape the fact that Catherine, who in her letters brought them into the atmosphere of divine love where her soul breathed the fire of charity, never lost sight of the state of their individual souls, their particular needs, their temptations, and their special difficulties. Thus, she made them realize that she was interested in them personally. As an example, let us cite a letter that she wrote to a woman of Perugia, who was notorious for her depraved life.

"Dearest daughter in Christ Jesus: I, Catherine, servant and slave of the servants of Jesus Christ, write to you in His precious blood in the desire of seeing you share in the blood of the Son of God, because without blood, life is impossible. Who are those who share in His blood? Those who live in the holy and sweet fear of God. He who fears God is ready to die rather than ever offend Him grievously. But, my daughter, I weep desolately at seeing that you, created in the image and likeness of God and redeemed by His precious blood, have no regard for your dignity nor for the great price you have cost Him. On the contrary, like the swine, you have reveled in impurity. You have made yourself the slave of sin; you have taken the devil for your master and you serve him day and night.

"Think how the master gives to his servant out of his own possessions. If you serve the devil you will share in his possessions. But what does the devil possess, my daughter? Only darkness, tempests, bitterness, pain, torments, and chastisements. Where he dwells there is nothing but weeping and gnashing of teeth and the loss of the beatific vision in which the happiness of the soul consists.

"Alas, is it possible that you have forgotten your Creator and that you have been reduced to the state of a member that is separated from His body and will at once wither away? Cut off and separated from Christ by mortal sin, you are like a dry branch that produces no fruit. Such a condition is the anticipation of hell in this life. Do you not see, my daughter, what slavery is yours and what wretchedness?

. . . Leave this dangerous slavery and the darkness in which you are living." [14]

To convince this public sinner, Catherine reminds her that we must die but that we know neither the day nor the hour of our death. It may come, as the Lord has said, "at the moment when we least expect it." Catherine reminds her of the terrible judgment that awaits her—eternal death in the company of the damned, fire and brimstone, the gnashing of teeth, the ever-gnawing worm of conscience, the remorse for having merited all this through her own fault, and the loss of the beatific vision of God by preferring the devil to Him. Such will be the fruits of her sinful life.

Then Catherine warns her that there is still time to save herself by doing holy violence to herself and by turning back to her Creator, who will accept her if she determines to abandon sin and return to the state of grace. "Believe me, my daughter, if you vomit the rottenness of your sins by confessing them with a firm purpose of never returning to your vomit, God will envelop you with His benevolence and will no longer remember that you have offended Him. Truly, this is the way God acts. He will never remember your sins. He will not punish in the next life those who here below punish themselves by repenting and hating their sins.

"Have recourse to sweet Mary, who is the Mother of pity and mercy. She will lead you into the presence of her Son, to whom she will show the breast that nourished Him, in order to induce Him to have mercy on you. Then, like a good daughter and a servant purchased by His blood, you will enter into the wounds of the Son of God where you will find such an ardent fire of ineffable love that it will burn and consume all your miseries and all your sins. I would that you bathe in His blood to wash away the leprosy of mortal

[14] Letter 276.

sin and all impurities in which you have lived for so long a time."

Catherine continues by urging her "dearest daughter" to imitate Magdalen in her repentance and penance and to carry her cross in imitation of Jesus Christ. "And if you protest that you shall have no means of livelihood, I assure you that God will provide. Besides, your own brother has promised me that he will give you whatever help you need. Do not wait for the judgment of God, which may very well fall on you if you do not become converted. . . . I shall say no more. Love Christ crucified. Realize that you must die and you do not know when. Remain in the holy and sweet love of God." [15]

This letter is an example of Catherine's apostolate. She used all her resources to snatch this soul from sin and to win it for Christ. She first greets the unfortunate woman with all tenderness by calling her "dearest daughter." Then she tries to arouse shame for her sins and to move her to repentance by describing the terrible consequences both here and hereafter. Above all, she insists on the possibility of forgiveness by reminding her of the love of God and the price—the shedding of His blood—that He paid for her redemption. God lovingly extends His arms and she has only to throw herself into them, as Magdalen did, by bathing in His precious blood. Let her invoke Mary, for the Mother of God knows how to move her Son to pity. But perhaps the change in her manner of living will cause her to die of hunger. No, says Catherine, for God Himself will provide for her needs. Her brother has already promised to come to her aid. One would have to possess a heart of stone or be positively blinded by sensuality to resist such solicitude.

When Catherine writes to the powerful ones of this world,

[15] *Ibid.*

to men of government, who also have in a sense the care of souls, her tone changes but her method remains the same. She reminds the Captain of the People of Siena (*Il Capitano del Popolo*) and those charged with the city's defense that the first condition for governing others well is to know how to govern oneself. If he lacks morality, a man in authority is poor and blind. Morality comes first. That was Catherine's motto in political affairs. The "wall of private life" was pointless in her eyes. Sooner or later, governments that lack a moral sense terminate by causing the worst political evil, subordinating the common good to their own selfish ends or to the interests of the party. Catherine says all this in her characteristic fashion, filling six pages with solid Christian doctrine and human psychology. She does not leave anything unsaid, nor does she try to soften her criticism. For example, she reminds the "esteemed gentlemen" that under their government evil ones are heard and the good are treated with contempt." [16]

When people had recourse to her in cases that did not concern her, she knew how to turn away these troublesome individuals but she would use the opportunity to remind them of salutary truths. A notary of Ustrigona, Christopher di Gano Guidini, who had a slight desire to become a monk but had renounced it for supposed family reasons, was thinking of marriage and a family. He wrote to Catherine to seek her advice in the choice of a bride, for he was hesitating as to which of three young women he should choose. Catherine let him know, first of all, that she was not deceived by the reasons he gave for remaining in the world and renouncing the life of perfection. Then turning to the question of his marriage and the advice he had sought, she said: "I do not willingly meddle in questions like this, which are more the

[16] Letter 121.

affair of seculars than of myself. However, since you wish it, here is my advice. As far as the situation of the three women is concerned, they are all good women. But if it does not matter to you that one of them has been married, choose her." According to Guidini's memoirs of Catherine, he does not seem to have understood the prudent lesson contained in this answer, which Catherine ends thus: "I beg the sovereign and eternal Charity to grant you what will be best for His honor and your salvation, and to both of you, the fullness of His grace and His eternal benediction. Remain in the holy love of God, sweet Jesus, Jesus, Love." [17]

REFORM OF THE CLERGY

In addition to the letters that Catherine wrote to laymen —chiefly to magistrates entrusted with the government of such important cities as Siena, Florence, Bologna, Perugia, and Pisa—and the letters addressed to Gregory XI, and Urban VI, and to cardinals and bishops, we also possess a great number that were sent to religious and priests. In these letters Catherine especially insists on their obligation to remain faithful to their vocation and to lead a truly priestly life, consecrated to the glory of God and the salvation of souls. She insisted on this so strongly because she knew from her own observation and had also learned directly from God that the clergy, both secular and religious, was faced with a crisis which could be averted only by a reform proportionate to the gravity of the situation.[18]

According to Raymond of Capua, in 1375, five years before the scandal broke, Catherine had predicted the Western Schism as the fatal result of this crisis of consciences and customs that had long been raging in the ranks of the clergy. She could foresee disaster as a result of the political dissen-

[17] *Letter* 43.   [18] Letter 12.

sions and civil wars, the departure of the popes to Avignon, the pagan spirit of the Renaissance, and the plague and famine—things which could never, in any country or at any time, promote self-control and asceticism, except among the saints. In that year, says Raymond, "the wickedness of many Italians had aroused to insurrection against Pope Gregory XI almost all the countries over which the Roman Church had incontestable rights. Catherine was then at Pisa and I was there with her. . . . When the revolt of Perugia was announced, the news filled my soul with great bitterness, for I saw clearly that there was no longer any fear of God or respect for the holy Church among Christians." [19]

Raymond's heart was so filled with sorrow that he wept as he told Catherine the news. "Don't weep so soon," she said, "for you will yet have many tears to shed. What you see now is milk and honey compared to that which will follow." When Raymond expressed astonishment at her words, Catherine added: "My Father, now it is the laity who act in this manner, but you will soon see the clergy do even worse things. . . . When the Roman Pontiff attempts to reform their morals, they will cause a universal scandal that will harass and divide the holy Church of God like the pestilence of heresy. It will not be a heresy properly speaking, but something very close to heresy—a division of the Church and of all Christendom. Fortify yourself with patience, for you will see these evils.

"When these trials and anguishes have passed," she added, "God will know how to purify his holy Church by means invisible to men. He will give new life to the spirit of His elect. He will bring about so great a reform in the Church of God and such a renewal of sanctity among its pastors that this thought alone makes my spirit rejoice in the Lord. As

[19] Cf. *Dialogue,* Chaps. CX–CXXXIV.

I have often told you, the Spouse of Christ, today disfigured and clothed in rags, will then be all beautiful, adorned with precious jewels and crowned with a diadem of all the virtues. The faithful will rejoice in the glory such holy pastors will bring them, and the unfaithful, attracted by the sweet odor of Jesus Christ, will return to the fold of Catholicism and to their true pastor, the Bishop of their souls."

Catherine, who was to live for only two years after the birth of the Great Schism and was to die before the great reform that followed, did not wait for the moral crisis of the clergy to attain its full development before exerting herself to correct the situation and find a suitable remedy. Her letters to popes, cardinals, bishops, and abbots give eloquent testimony of this. These letters are so well known that only a few extracts are necessary to reveal the full extent of her apostolic method. The following excerpt is from a letter to Peter d'Estaing, Cardinal of Ostia, named papal legate to Bologna by Gregory XI, after having been named governor of the patrimony of the Holy See and of the Papal States in Italy by Urban V.

"It seems to me, dearest Father, that it is time to give glory to God. You are now in charge of temporal and spiritual things. . . . As for the temporal, be courageous and strive as much as you can for peace and unity in the land. . . . I am persuaded that if you put on the new man of Christ, sweet Jesus, and strip yourself of the old man, which is your sensual nature, you will accomplish all that I prescribe, for you will be freed of all servile fear. . . . God has placed you in a position that requires only one kind of fear. That is why I have told you I wish to find you courageous and not a cowardly man. I hope that the divine goodness will grant you the grace to accomplish His Will, which is your desire and mine."

In a similar vein she writes to the Abbot of Sant' Antimo: "Put all your care in showing yourself to be a good pastor and a good gardener—a good pastor by correcting and a good gardener by ploughing the earth, changing disorder into order, rooting out vice, and, as much as possible with the help of divine and sweet grace, planting virtue, which grows abundantly in the soul that hungers for God." [20]

During this same period the papal political affairs were represented in Italy by another French prelate, Gerard du Puy, Abbot of Marmoutiers and a nephew of Gregory XI. He enjoyed the confidence of Gregory XI and wished to act as an intermediary between Catherine and the Pope, as he had done previously in the case of St. Birgitta, the Swedish mystic who died in 1373. He wrote to Catherine, placing himself at her service. Catherine answered with a long letter in which she shows how anxious she was to see that those who could do so should work for the reform of the clergy. As always, she begins by reminding him of the doctrine of love: the transformation of the soul through conformity to Christ and the destruction of self-will in the sacred fire of the divine will. Then she proceeds to give practical advice with the liberty of expression that is characteristic of her and which astonishes those who have forgotten or who never knew that these letters were dictated during her ecstasies, when she was in full contemplation, and that she was speaking in the name of God.

"I received your letter with great pleasure," she says, "and it was a deep consolation for me to know that you have not forgotten such a vile and wretched creature as myself. Here is the way in which I would answer your three questions: I think it would be well for the Pope, our sweet Christ on earth, to free himself from two things that corrupt the Bride

[20] Letter 11.

of Christ. The first is the excessive affection he bears his family, about whom he is far too solicitous. . . . The second is an excessive sweetness that springs from a too indulgent nature. Alas, alas, the members of Christ are corrupting because no one chastises them. The three detestable vices that our Lord especially abominates are the impurity, avarice, and pride which are prevalent among priests, who think only of pleasures and feasting and are concerned only with amassing wealth. They watch unmoved as the demons of hell snatch the souls that have been confided to their care, for they themselves are voracious wolves and traffic in divine grace. A firm hand is needed to put order here, for too much mercy is sometimes the greatest cruelty. I pray God that the Holy Father will suppress that exaggerated affection for his family; but I have faith in the glorious future that has been predicted for him. Goodness will not triumph until corruption has reached its plenitude." [21]

So much for the Pope; but Catherine also has something to say to the nephew. Gerard had thought it well to give Catherine to understand that he was a great sinner, and she takes him at his word. "God does not will the death of the sinner," she tells him, "but that he should be converted and live . . . and I, your most unworthy daughter, shall take upon myself the debt of your sins and shall burn yours and mine at the same time in the furnace of divine love. Rest assured that God in His mercy will pardon you; but put forth every effort henceforth to lead a new life."

After this preamble of lofty inspiration and delicate tact, Catherine, who did not forget that she was writing to the nephew and the confidant of the Pope, proceeds to speak to him without any circumspection. "You ought," she tells him, "to work with the Holy Father as well as you are able

[21] Letter 109.

to drive out the bad shepherds, who are wolves and devils incarnate and think of nothing but sumptuous fare, luxurious palaces, and beautiful equipages. Alas, that which Christ earned on the wood of the cross is now wasted on women of pleasure. Though it should cost you your life, I bid you tell the Holy Father to put an end to such great scandal. And when the time comes for him to appoint cardinals and other shepherds of the Church, beg him not to let himself be influenced by flattery, cupidity, or simony, and not to consider whether those concerned are nobles or commoners, for virtue and good reputation ennoble a man before God." [22]

This letter was written around 1375, shortly before Gregory XI created nine new cardinals, among them his own nephew, the Abbot of Marmoutiers, the very one Catherine had asked to intercede with the Pope that he name cardinals known for their virtue and their good reputation. We do not know whether Gerard du Puy delivered Catherine's message to the Pope, but if he did, it does not seem that Gregory paid much attention to it, although personally he held Catherine in high esteem. He seems to have been motivated more by political than religious reasons, for out of the nine cardinals created, seven were French, one was Spanish, and one, Italian. On the other hand, we know that Gregory XI was naturally timid but had a deeply religious spirit. If his hands had not been tied, he would surely have heeded Catherine's advice. But at that time politics dominated everything and the Pope would have needed Catherine's sanctity and iron will to ignore political issues and create cardinals renowned for their virtue rather than their political value or diplomatic qualities.

[22] *Ibid.*

However, even if we suppose that the Abbot of Marmoutiers neglected to deliver Catherine's message to the Pope, Gregory XI received a personal letter from her after the naming of the nine cardinals. Catherine does not conceal her frame of mind. "I have heard here," she writes to him from Pisa, "that you have created cardinals. I believe that the honor of God and the interests of the Church demand that you should never appoint any but virtuous men. To act otherwise would be a serious offence against God and injurious to the Church. Then it should not be surprising if God chastises us; this is only just. I beg you to do your duty manfully and in the fear of God.

"I have also learned that you would like to confer another office on our Master General. If this is true, I beg you, by the love of Christ crucified, to do all in your power to give us a good and virtuous Vicar. Our Order needs one, for it has fallen into decline. You can consult on this matter with Nicholas da Osimo and the Archbishop of Otranto. For my part, I shall also write to them.

"Remain in the sweet and holy love of God. I humbly ask your blessing and beg you to pardon the presumption with which I have written to you." [23]

This letter to the Pope scandalized Jorgensen. Evidently, as he observes, Francis of Assisi would never have spoken to anyone in such a tone, especially to a pope. But that proves absolutely nothing, except that a century later in the Church of God, the vocation of St. Catherine was not that of St. Francis. One could not imagine St. Francis confronting the "Scourge of God" if he had lived in the time of Attila, like St. Genevieve of Paris or St. Leo the Great, to command him in the name of God to turn back. Manners

[23] Letter 185.

change with the times. Each has his role in the Church, according to the designs of divine providence.

It is an absurdity to explain Catherine's spirited attitude, as it appears in her letters to cardinals, apostolic nuncios, and even to the Pope himself, by appealing only to her feminine temperament, her domineering spirit, or, one would almost say, her pride and presumption. "Catherine of Siena is a woman," Jorgensen tells us. "What she thinks is, of course, right. Hence the unity, the absolutism of her life. . . . Catherine leads the exiled papacy by her firm and fearless little hand back to Rome. For in all the world there is only one competent person, only one who is right —and that one is herself. . . . She was absolutely sure of herself. It never occurred to her that she might be wrong." [24]

Thus speaks Jorgensen, an intelligent and deeply religious soul, but one who finds any display of authority naturally repugnant. He confused the decisive mind of Catherine in practical matters with a domineering spirit she never possessed. He did not understand at all—as he acknowledges in the preface of his book—the will of Catherine, that legendary *"Io voglio,"* which aimed first at control of herself, to conquer her own passions, because such was the will of God and which, for the same reason, only in the name of God and not her own, she imposed on others when her conscience demanded it.

Haunted by the gentle St. Francis, Jorgensen judged Catherine through a comparison with Francis when he wished to explain her exceptionally strong will. This is the error of his judgment. Moreover, he ought to have remembered that all those who knew St. Catherine and associated with her were as charmed by her sweetness, her humility,

[24] Jorgensen, *op. cit.,* p. 214.

and her unfaltering patience as they were by her energetic will. Threfore, her strong will should be explained otherwise than by the good opinion she had of herself as a woman and the certainty she felt of never being mistaken or of being the only person in the world capable of bringing the Pope back to Rome.

But Jorgensen ought especially to have remembered that Catherine dictated her letters during her ecstasies, when she was united with God in contemplation, engulfed in the vision of love, and illumined by divine wisdom from whom she took her words. When she descended from Tabor and plunged into action, she retained the divine light and judged things from God's point of view. The influence of the gift of wisdom permeated her counsels and as a result, her prudence was necessarily more clairvoyant and imperious.

In a word, Catherine left the divine union with a hunger for absolute moral truth, a perfect accuracy of vision, and an irresistible urge to conform her decisions with the demands of wisdom and divine love.

She had learned from God the lamentable state in which the clergy was living, to the detriment of so many souls whom Jesus had redeemed at the price of His blood. How could she remain unmoved before such a sight, when Jesus Himself had made her leave her cell to collaborate with Him principally in the reform of the clergy? How could she be silent on this important point when writing to the Pope, on whom this reform depended directly through the creation of virtuous shepherds who would be devoted body and soul to their divine task?

No human consideration could stop her nor cause her to veil the truth, nor even to soften its utterance when, on the contrary, the only way she had of moving the Pope and of persuading him to thrust the red hot iron into the wound was to speak to him bluntly, in the name of God. Catherine well knew that from a human point of view she was audacious. The proof of this is that at the end of her letter to Gregory XI she asks pardon for her presumption. But she was not taking the human viewpoint when she wrote to him. She was simply transmitting a divine message and she wrote to him at the dictation of God, under the inspiration of the Holy Ghost and in the light of His wisdom. One can be certain that Gregory XI felt this and that he read Catherine's letters in the same spirit. If he had been convinced it was not a saint who wrote to him in this manner, but a simple woman who was too sure of herself and too confident of her own opinion, he would not have permitted her to write him a second time and surely he would not have permitted her to come to Avignon. Even if she had come of her own initiative, he would not have given her an audience, as we know he did with such kindness and trust, precisely to find out from her what God wished of him.

THE CRUSADE

With the same zeal that Catherine endeavored to propagate in Italy the idea of a reform of the clergy, she attempted to rally the hesitant to the idea of a Crusade. Since the end of the thirteenth century, when the Holy Places and all of Palestine had been taken by the Sultan Bibars, a Momeluke adventurer who had become ruler of Egypt, and when Acre and all Syria were taken by his successors, the Western princes resigned themselves to the catastrophe that nullified all the heroic efforts of the thirteenth century and abandoned the idea of a general Crusade. In the Orient the Christians held only Cyprus, Armenia, and a few principalities of the Latin Empire. In 1344 a Christian fleet took possession of Smyrna, but Humbert, Dauphin of Vienna, who had been at the head of the Crusade, made no use of this success. Peter de Lusignan, King of Cyprus, took Armenia in 1361, and at the urging of his chancellor, Philip de Mézières, conducted an enthusiastic campaign for a general Crusade among the princes of the West from 1362 to 1365. He was well received but had to carry on almost alone and content himself with alarming the Moslems with foolhardy surprise attacks, seizing Alexandria in 1365 and pillaging the ports of Syria in 1367.

At this period the popes sojourned at Avignon and had to face immense difficulties both in the religious and political order. They certainly did not abandon the idea of a Crusade for liberating the Holy Places from the Moslem yoke. Clement VI, Innocent VI, Urban V, and Gregory XI took up the projects abandoned by Benedict XII. But the ultimate success of projects of such huge scope remained subordinate, in their opinion, to that of the reconciliation of the kings of England and France, the eventual heads of the Crusade. That is why the Popes clung so obstinately to the re-establishment of peace before preaching the Crusade and urging the princes of the West and their Christian nations to launch one.

Under such conditions what could Catherine do? Blessed Raymond, to whom it is always necessary to turn in order to have the testimony of a scrupulous witness in these delicate matters, is indignant that Catherine's words and actions have been distorted. It has been asserted that she announced a Crusade of all Christendom against the Moslems (which never took place) and that she promised that she would take part in it with her disciples.

"It is true," says Raymond, "that the Saint always wanted the Crusade and worked energetically for the realization of her desire. In some ways it is the main reason she went to Avignon to see Pope Gregory XI. She wished to urge him to organize a Crusade. I was a witness and in my presence she used all possible arguments. I remember one day in particular when she was most insistent on this subject with the Sovereign Pontiff. I was present at the conversation because I served as interpreter between the Pope, who spoke in Latin, and our virgin, who spoke in the Tuscan dialect.

"The Pontiff had answered: 'We must first make peace and then we shall organize the Crusade.' To which she replied: 'Holy Father, you will never find a better means than the Crusade for establishing peace among Christians. All these men of war who are engaged in fighting among the faithful will gladly go to fight in the service of God. Few men are so wicked as not to render wholeheartedly to God a service that is pleasant to themselves and is at the same time a means of satisfying for their sins. Once the discord is extinguished, the conflagration will cease. Thus, Holy Father, with one blow you will obtain several excellent results: you will give Christians the peace for which they are begging; in losing those military men who are imprisoned in the snares of their sins you will save them; if they bring back a victory, you will intervene with other Christian princes to consolidate their successes; and if they fall in battle, you will have won for Jesus Christ souls that today seem destined for perdition. From this Crusade three good results will emerge: peace for Christendom, repentance for the soldiers, and the salvation of many Saracens!' "

After reporting this magnificent conversation of Catherine with the Pope, Raymond insists that never, either in private or in public, had he heard Catherine say when the Crusade would take place. On the contrary, he always found her very reticent on this point, avoiding an answer to his precise questions. In that matter, as in all others, Catherine had complete trust in divine providence.

"It is true," Raymond adds, "that she often spoke of the Crusade and that she encouraged as many as she could to take part. She expressed the hope that the Lord, casting a glance of pity on His people, would save many souls of the faithful as well as of the infidels through this holy war. But no one can state truthfully that she indicated the time of this Crusade or promised that she would take part in it with her disciples."

In 1373, three years before Catherine went to Avignon (June 18, 1376), Gregory XI himself had called the Christians to a Crusade and Catherine had enthusiastically joined the movement. The Holy Father had made her promise to pray for him and for the Church, and as a sign of his benevolence, had granted her an indulgence. She had answered Gregory's oral message with a letter in which she asked permission to deliver her body to all kinds of suffering, through love of the sweet Blood, and she begged the supreme and eternal Truth to give her the grace to immolate herself for this holy cause.

But the wind was not in favor of Crusades. What could Catherine do against the ill will of the princes, the weakness of the Pope, and the lethargy of Christian nations? Alone, or almost alone, she fought to keep the project so dear to her from falling into oblivion, because to its realization were attached the glory of God and the salvation of souls. Never had she set her will with so much fervor and insistence to arouse people from their inertia.

Basically, Gregory XI remained sympathetic to the idea of a Crusade. But failing to find a prince who would consent to recruit troops and lead them into the Holy Land, he had to postpone the project until after the re-establishment of peace between France and England. She had scarcely arrived at Avignon when Catherine, who knew the mind of the Sovereign Pontiff on this question, took it upon herself to find a prince who would consent to lead the Crusade. She visited the Duke of Anjou, who had been sent by his brother, Charles V of France, at the instigation of the cardinals, to keep the Pope from returning to Rome. Catherine was careful not to speak of the Duke's mission, for in her soul she could not approve. But by her burning words she won him over to the cause of the Crusade. The Duke even went so far as to promise to equip an army at his own expense, provided the King of France consented.

Catherine also wrote to the King and in the same tone as she wrote to popes, nuncios, and cardinals when the salvation of souls was at stake. Faithful to her apostolic method, she said to Charles V: "I beg you and I will you to follow Jesus crucified and that you love the salvation of your neighbor. . . . I am astonished that you are not willing to sacrifice all temporal things and even your very life when you see the loss of so many souls, the death of so many people, and so many religious, women, and children persecuted and homeless because of this war (against the English). . . . I tell you in the name of Jesus crucified, do not delay in making peace. Make peace and turn your weapons against the infidels. Devote yourself to unfurling and defending the standard of the holy Cross." [25]

Then she comes to the purpose of her letter. "It seems to me," she writes, "that your brother, the Duke of Anjou, wishes to consecrate himself to this holy cause for the love

[25] Letter 235.

of Christ. Would you want to be responsible for preventing him? No, you will follow the footsteps of Jesus crucified, and you will accomplish His will and mine." [26]

At the same time that she wrote to the King, she informed the Pope that the Duke of Anjou was quite willing to lead the Crusade. Unfortunately, it was no longer the time when kings and Christian nations were willing to subordinate their temporal interests to the safeguarding of spiritual interests. The thought of dying in the act of liberating the sepulcher of Christ no longer moved their hearts and the burning exhortations of Catherine found no echo.

At least Catherine had done her duty. She had knocked at every door without being discouraged. The deliverance of the Holy Places did not depend on her. If she could have mobilized the devil and all his legions, she would probably not have hesitated to do so. Actually, in 1375 she tried to rally to the cause of the Crusade recently preached by Gregory XI in his bull of July 1, 1375, that tool of the devil, John Hawkwood, the formidable English freelancer who headed a band of mercenaries and was threatening to invade Tuscany.

Hawkwood—*Aguto* as the Italians called him, trying to pronounce his difficult name—was then at Pisa. One morning the sentries outside Hawkwood's camp were not a little surprised to see two Dominicans approach and ask to speak with *Aguto*. When the friars were led to the Englishman, they gave him a parchment from Catherine. "Dearest and sweetest brother in Christ Jesus," she wrote. "It is high time that you enter into yourself a little and consider the sufferings and torments that you have endured in serving the devil. My soul desires that you change your manner of life

[26] *Ibid.*

and that you and your companions enroll yourselves under the cross of Christ crucified in order to form a company of Christ and wage war against the infidel dogs who hold the Holy Places, where the supreme Truth suffered death for us and was buried. I beg you, in the name of Christ Jesus, to war against the infidels, since you delight so much in warring." [27]

At first sight, one is astonished that Catherine should ask the leader of the mercenaries, known for his murder and rapine, to become all at once a "knight of Christ" and to prefer an unprofitable war against the infidels to the one he was planning to carry on in Tuscany in order to gather provisions for his troops at the expense of the citizens. Catherine knew that this notorious *condottiere* had already promised Urban V in 1365 to engage in a Crusade and had failed to fulfill his promise, but she made a new attempt. The fact of the matter is that Hawkwood was moved by Catherine's letter and Raymond, the bearer of the letter, did not leave the camp until all the chiefs and Hawkwood himself had taken an oath to march against the infidels. They signed this promise by their own hands and affixed their seals.

Naturally, Hawkwood did not keep this oath made to Catherine any more than he had kept the one previously made to Urban V. Nevertheless, it is not a little surprising to see that later on he came to the aid of the Pope against his chief enemy, Bernabò Visconti. "It was a moment," remarks Jorgensen," when he was again under the influence of her who had once called him her 'dearest and sweetest brother in Christ Jesus.' " [28]

[27] Letter 140.   [28] Jorgensen, *op. cit.*, p. 208.

AVIGNON AND ROME

To complete this over-all view of Catherine's apostolate and apostolic method, we have yet to speak briefly of her intervention in the matter of the return of Pope Gregory XI to Rome. Here especially we must guard against all exaggeration. It would certainly be excessive to maintain, as certain panegyrists did in her day, that it was she who determined the return of Gregory XI to Rome. It would likewise be exaggeration, less regrettable, to claim with those who for political reasons wanted the Pope to remain at Avignon, that Catherine could not be held responsible even in the smallest way for his "unfortunate" return to the Eternal City. The truth lies somewhere between these two extremes and it is favorable enough to Catherine so that we are not tempted to alter it to her advantage.

When Catherine arrived at Avignon on June 18, 1376, she met Raymond and several of her most devoted disciples who had preceded her, among them John Tantucci di Lecceto and Neri di Landoccio. She went to Avignon, as Raymond tells us, to talk to the Pope about the Crusade and also to talk to him about his return to Rome. Gregory XI knew Catherine by reputation. We have seen that in order to facilitate her constantly increasing apostolate, he had authorized three confessors to accompany her and had granted them the full powers or faculties of bishops.

Besides, Catherine had written to him about the Florentines, who had formed a league against the Pope and had asked her to intercede with Gregory XI to make peace with them. According to the letter she wrote from Avignon on June 28, after her first audience with the Pope, to the "Eight of War" at Florence, Gregory XI was quite disposed to make peace. But he did not trust the good faith of the

Florentines, who had actually sent ambassadors to him at Avignon, but only to quiet his suspicions. These three ambassadors represented a new government that did not even wish to hear the word "peace" mentioned. They categorically refused the mediation of Catherine. This refusal is a compliment to the saintly ambassadress, for they feared her apostolic method as well as the extraordinary influence she would not fail to exert on them as she did on the Pope in the interests of a peace which they did not want at any price. Catherine then devoted herself entirely to her task par excellence—to hasten the Pope's return to Rome.

Bartholomew Dominici, who was also at Avignon, gives a report of Catherine's first conversation with Gregory XI on this delicate matter. He had decided to return to the Eternal City, but he hesitated to do so. Moreover, everything seemed to give added cause for hesitation: the King of France, because the Pope's stay at Avignon suited his political plans; the cardinals, because their tranquil life on the banks of the Rhone deterred them from returning to a country such as Italy, which was ravaged by civil wars; the prospect of a journey that had been represented to the Pope as dangerous; and a sojourn at Rome that could hardly be peaceful at the head of a clergy that needed reform and surrounded by rebellious states he would have to appease.

When Catherine appeared before him, Gregory asked her what she thought of his return to the Eternal City. Catherine humbly excused herself by saying it was not proper that a "weak woman" such as herself should give advice to the Sovereign Pontiff. But the Pope answered: "I do not ask your advice, but that, in the name of holy obedience, you tell me the will of God." Humbly bowing her head, Catherine, who could read souls, answered: "Who knows better than Your Holiness, for you have made a vow to return to Rome." Gregory was stupefied at this reply, for no one else in the world knew of this vow.

He then decided to set out for Rome. But that alone was not sufficient; Catherine had to return to the matter several times in order to help him conquer his doubts. She had to fight against all sorts of traps that were laid for her. The cardinals tried to stop her from seeing the Pope; three inquisitors questioned her about her ecstasies, her continual fast, and her doctrine. It took all of Catherine's presence of mind and a strong will to keep her head and finally to silence them. Her victory was so complete that the three inquisitors became her devoted friends. She found in the Pope himself a powerful refuge against her enemies.

Catherine's influence over the Pope's hesitant will grew with time and the departure from Avignon seemed imminent when the King of France sent his brother, the Duke of Anjou, to try to offset Catherine's influence. When the Duke realized that the Pope obeyed only Catherine on the question of leaving Avignon, he resolved to bring Catherine to his point of view. He merely wasted his breath. As a matter of fact, just the contrary happened: Catherine persuaded him to lead a Crusade. But he could get no help from her in keeping the Pope at Avigon. On this point agreement was impossible. The Duke, in the name of the King of France, wanted to keep the Pope at Avignon for political reasons; Catherine wished his return to Rome for spiritual reasons. It was Catherine who carried the day. As always, she resorted to her apostolic method, which drew its inspiration solely from the glory of God and the salvation of souls. On this plane she was invincible.

Not content with the influence she exerted over the Pope by direct speech, she sent him a series of letters in which she refuted the objections of all those cardinals and Christian princes who were opposed to the departure of Gregory XI. The Pope informed Catherine of these objections through Raymond of Capua or Thomas di Petra, his notary. We shall cite only one letter, the most moving, in which the apostolate of Catherine appears in all its brilliance and her apostolic method in all its strength. What could carry weight with an irresolute but deeply religious Pope: the advice or threats of men interested in his stay at Avignon for human reasons, or the personal disinterestedness of a saint who spoke the language of faith and common sense and found in her love of God and the Holy Church an irresistible accent of authority to beg him to hasten his return to the Eternal City?

"Holiest and most blessed Father in Christ, sweet Jesus," she writes to him. "Your unworthy and miserable daughter Catherine encourages you in His precious blood, in the desire of seeing you delivered from all servile fear, for the timid soul loses all the strength of good resolutions and holy desires. Therefore, I will pray the good and sweet Jesus to despoil you of all servile fear and to leave in you only a holy fear. May the fire of charity burn in you so that you will not be able to hear the voices of the incarnate devils who, from what I learn, wish to place obstacles to your return by suggesting, in order to frighten you, that you will be surrendering yourself to certain death. I say to you in the name of Christ crucified, most sweet and holy Father, that you have no cause for fear. Come in all confidence and trust in Christ, sweet Jesus. If you do your duty, God will protect you and no one can prevail against you.

"Courage, Father; be a man! I say to you that you have nothing to fear. But if you neglect to do your duty, then indeed you have cause to fear. It is your duty to come to Rome; therefore come. Come in peace, without any fear.

And if anyone tries to prevent you, then say boldly what Christ said to St. Peter, who out of the tenderness of his love wished Him to avoid the Passion: 'Get thee behind Me, Satan! Thou art a scandal unto Me, because thou savorest not the things that are of God, but the things that are of men. Is it not necessary that I do the will of My Father?'

"So do you likewise, dearest Father. Imitate Him whose Vicar you are and say to all those around you: 'Though I should lose my life a thousand times, yet will I do the will of my Father!'. . . . Let them say what they wish, but remain firm in your holy resolve. My Father, Brother Raymond, has asked me in your name to pray to God in order to learn whether your return to Rome would raise any difficulties. I have just prayed, both before and after Holy Communion, and I have not seen either death or any other danger, of which certain people have told you." [29]

Certain persons had convinced Gregory XI that by leaving Avignon he would encounter the worst dangers, that he would be shipwrecked or poisoned. But the will of God finally triumphed and Gregory XI re-entered the Eternal City. Catherine's apostolic vocation was ended.

Elsewhere we have recounted how, after the premature but natural death of Gregory XI, his successor, Urban VI, was lawfully elected and the election was uncontested. Then, because of influences due partly to his irascible temperament but still more to political reasons, the Great Western Schism broke out. Powerless to avert this deadly peril, but trusting in divine mercy, Catherine, who had learned from God and announced to Raymond of Capua that the Church would one day emerge triumphant from this cruel

[29] Letter 233.

trial, thought only of suffering and of dying for this Church that she loved so deeply.

Summoned to Rome by Urban VI, she died there on January 29, 1380, after a long and painful agony, telling her sorrowing disciples: "My dearest and sweetest children, be assured that if I die now, it is because I have immolated and offered up my life for the holy Church and I consider this a special grace. Do not be sorrowful, but rejoice exceedingly, seeing that I am passing from this place of sorrow to rest in the ocean of peace which is God eternal and to be united with my sweetest Spouse."

Then, like her Father St. Dominic on his death bed, surrounded by his sons, she added: "I promise that I shall always be near you and shall be more useful to you up there than I could ever have been in this world, for I am leaving the darkness to go into eternal light." Time has confirmed this prophecy.

EPILOGUE

Does the portrait which we have just sketched resemble St. Catherine? Competent critics who knew her better than we, through having studied her for a long time, and who read these pages before they were sent to the printer, say that it is. God grant they are not mistaken!

Whatever may be the truth of the matter, to complete this sketch it was necessary to guard against two pitfalls that many historians—panegyrists or unwitting detractors—have not always avoided. The first is the attempt to explain Catherine's extraordinary life and apostolate in terms of her natural talents of mind and heart, amplified and made fruitful, as they say, by a delicate but excessive, if not unhealthy, sensitivity. The second consists in exaggerating the supernatural aspect of her interior life and apostolate, delighting in the enumeration of all the prodigies—visions, ecstasies, miracles, and prophecies—that accompanied her life and work; seeing the supernatural in everything, even in the simple things of her daily life; in a word, absorbing the natural in the supernatural to the point of making Catherine unapproachable and almost non-human.

We have made every effort to avoid this double error that tends either to humanize Catherine excessively or to dehumanize her. We believe that the truth lies between these two extremes, as is shown by her actions as well as her writings. Grace and nature are manifested in brilliant harmony, each performing its function, but without destroying the equilibrium.

This Saint, who apparently lived in a supramundane world, never lost contact with the earth. She lived in God, but at the same time in the midst of men. She was preoccupied with the heavenly fatherland, but that of the earth—her Italy, Tuscany, and Siena—also had a place in her heart. The Holy Ghost inspired her in all things and lavished His gifts upon her, but that did not cause her to lose her common sense. She loved God above all things, it is true, but she found in this very love the superhuman strength to love her neighbor and to compassionate with him in his pains and miseries as well as to share in his joys. This young woman of vigorous health but delicate sensitivity, for the love of Jesus Christ and sinners, inflicted on herself such penances as would make the most insensible person shudder. But when others were concerned, she showed great prudence and was grieved to see them suffer. This child, who could neither read nor write, received from God a spiritual doctrine at once deep and certain, and she assimilated it to such a degree that when dictating to her followers, she seems to have composed it naturally and drawn it from her own soul. This holy religious, enclosed in her cell so long in prayer, meditation, and contemplation, became the accepted counselor of princes, kings, and popes. She seemed to be interested only in the things of the next world, yet no one proved more capable of managing the affairs of this world than she.

At the dawn of the Renaissance, when the fame of Petrarch was becoming widespread, Catherine, without the least literary interest, dictated to her secretaries hundreds of letters that are masterpieces of style and which, to quote the most competent writers, mark a period of history of the Italian language.

Catherine's originality and power of attraction consist precisely in that harmonious balance of the natural and supernatural gifts she had received from God. Without effort or affectation, she used these gifts with an incomparable mastery and spontaneity. Happy those who approached her, even though they were the most hardened sinners. They would ultimately fall into her net and admit that they were conquered. An extraordinary charm emanated from her, an irresistible attraction. In spite of her penances and all her physical and spiritual trials, her illness, and her preoccupations of all kinds, she preserved an imperturbable calm. Her expression remained affable, her words, simple and moving. One had the impression that she was never disturbed; that she was all things to all. Whatever anyone asked, she gave, and more. And behind this attractive exterior, so profoundly human, was an inexhaustible love of God, a kind of incandescent flame in which her exceptional will was forged, that will which was capable of all gentleness but which, when necessary, imposed itself on all with great firmness: *Io voglio!* What marvelous balance in the midst of a world torn by hate and flowing with rivers of blood!

Such is the Saint we offer to the men of our time, a time similar to that which Catherine knew, but even worse because hatred is deeper and more universal and blood flows in still greater torrents. May this Saint draw to herself all those men and women who suffer from the lack of harmony between mind and heart. May she attract those souls who have turned away from God and who, enclosed in the infernal circle of their passions, want to get out but cannot find the way. May she give sight to the blind, hearing to the deaf, speech to the mute—all the unfortunates who today have become insensible to the light and the word of God. With their bodies satiated with earthly pleasures, they feel more or less consciously the need to drink from higher and purer springs and to quench their thirst and ultimately to taste that water which, as Christ told the Samaritan woman, becomes, "a fountain of water, springing up into life everlasting." [30]

Catherine promised all her Dominican brothers and sisters that she would be still more useful to them in heaven than on earth. We would wish that her protection extend farther than the Dominican Order. In the terrible times in which we live and with an eye to the approaching spiritual restoration of the world, may her care extend to all those who are stifling in the atmosphere of passion and hate and grant them finally to breathe the purified air of love.

[30] John 4:14.